Stephen Karcher Ph.D., is an internationally known scholar, writer, translator, lecturer and consultant. He was Director of Research at the Eranos Foundation from 1988–1994 and guided the evolution of their I Ching Project, pioneering a new approach to the practice of divination. He has published many books, translations and scholarly articles in the field of mythology, comparative religion, depth psychology and divination and the varieties of spiritual experience. He was a professional dancer and choreographer for several years, and holds a doctorate in Comparative Literature and Archetypal Psychology.

T0312580

THE I CHING
PLAIN AND SIMPLE

A Guide to Working
with the Oracle of Change

STEPHEN KARCHER

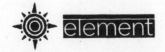

Element
An Imprint of HarperCollins*Publishers*
77–85 Fulham Palace Road,
Hammersmith, London W6 8JB

The website address is: www.thorsonselement.com

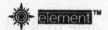

and *Element* are trademarks of
HarperCollins*Publishers* Limited

First published in Great Britain in 1997
by Element Books Limited
This edition published by Element 2004

A catalogue record of this book
is available from the British Library

ISBN 0-00-733258-0

Contents

Acknowledgements

I would like to dedicate this book to Jean-Louis and Maryke Boele van Hensbroek in appreciation of their kindness, understanding and inspiration. Thanks, too, to Ian Fenton, who suffered through many a change.

Foreword

The modern world thinks that change is objective and predictable. We use statistics and norms to describe it, and pretend it is the same for everyone. The old world saw things differently, recognizing change and chance as the work of the spirit. Divination and its symbols are a key to this world. They are used to connect the hidden powers creating change to an individual's life.

This symbolic approach can help you deal with the changes in *your* life, just as it helps people in traditional cultures. It can resolve fears and uncertainties and give practical advice on everyday problems. It gives the spirit a 'voice' in your daily life.

The *I Ching* is one of the world's oldest and most profound divination systems, a powerful tool which can help you navigate the voyage of your life. It helps you to see the forces that are shaping difficult situations, and to understand the meaning of obstacles. It keeps you connected to the creative process of life. It brings out your helping spirit, the inner voice that helps you find your way.

This book is meant for those people who want to use the *I Ching* to work with the changes in their lives. It describes the world of symbols that the *I Ching* creates, and includes practical instructions on forming questions and simple ways to get an answer. The 64 'chapters' or Figures of the *I Ching* are given in a clear new translation that retains the direct, yet mysterious, quality of the original. Take time to read through the introduction, be prepared to learn a few new things, and soon you will be consulting the oldest oracle in the world.

The *I Ching* has been a spiritual guide and a very real help in times of danger for many people in the 3,000 years it has existed. Personally, I feel a very deep gratitude for its presence in my life and in the lives of those I care for. I sincerely hope that something of this comes through to you in this book, and that you, too, may experience the friendship of this spirit.

PART ONE
The World of Change

The World of Change

Change is the very essence of living. Our lives change, our dreams change, the seasons change, our world changes. Some changes are predictable, some unpredictable. Some are sought after, some avoided. Some bring joy, others bring grief and sorrow. The *I Ching* is an attempt to understand and work with change. But it does not *describe* change; it *participates* in change. It shows the way change occurs because it is *part of the process it models*. By using it, you participate in change rather than being its unconscious victim.

THE ORIGINS OF THE I CHING

A Book and an Oracle

The *I Ching* is first of all a book. It was treasured as a key to the mystery of transformation. It was elaborated and interpreted over 3,000 years of Chinese history.

The book consists of 64 Chapters or Figures that are a combination of linear diagrams and short, vivid, mysterious sayings. We might call them the 64 Shapes of Change. But, unlike other books, you do not simply read the *I Ching*. You ask it questions and it gives you answers. For the *I Ching* is more than a book: it is an oracle. It 'speaks' to your situation. It gives you a mirror of the hidden forces at work in the changes you are confronting.

Bamboo Shamans

Most of the words used in the *I Ching* grew out of an oral tradition of songs, chants, sayings, omens and symbolic events used by the shamans and diviners of ancient China. The written words first appear carved on 'oracle bones', prepared tortoise shells and ox shoulder bones used in divination by fire. They were later collected into 'Books of *I*', written on thin slats of bamboo. The use of these texts was carefully guarded and the diviners who used them were called 'bamboo shamans'. This sort of oracular consultation reflects a particular approach to the experience of the spirit.

CONNECTING TO THE SPIRIT WORLD THROUGH ORACLES AND DIVINATION

Oracles and divination are not sorcery. They are an inner process that can show what is at work in your unconscious. The ancient world called this unconscious the world of the spirits. It is like the ocean of images you sometimes see in your dreams, where you are 'unconsciously' connected to other people and things.

Oracles and divination can show us this hidden side of our lives. They can mirror the spiritual and psychological forces that are at work behind the scenes of our lives. But oracles are about questions, so rather than describing what they do, let us ask a simple question and imagine the sort of answer we might get. The question is: 'What time is it?'

A Special Kind of Time

In normal life we look at the clock for an answer to this question. According to the dictionary, the clock shows us a particular kind of time, a 'non-spatial continuum in which events occur and a system by which such intervals are measured'. The units of this time are identical and interchangeable. One minute, hour or day is like any other. So we get an answer like 12:35, 17 July 1997. If two different people ask the question at the same time, they will get the same answer.

However, when we turn to an oracle, we learn about a different kind of time. The answer to our question might be something like this: the time of your life, the right time, the moment of truth, time out, behind the times, making time, bedtime, doing time, keeping time, in time, out of time. All these expressions give an individual quality to time that *depends upon the person asking the question.* If two people ask this question at the same time, they will get quite different answers.

Now, we all experience both these kinds of time, but we see them as *incommensurate.* One goes on inside us, the other goes on outside us. Historians of science have called this split in time the 'disenchantment of the world'. It marks the point where myth, imagination and spirit were split off from what we now call 'scientific reality'.

Putting Time Back Together

The old world, however, the world before its 'disenchantment', told time differently. It 'told' you into a *story* of the time by connecting your experience with images and symbols. These images represent forces in the unconscious that *connect* the inner and the outer worlds.

This interconnection comes through imagining. It characterizes what we usually call 'superstition' or 'pre-scientific thinking'. For, in our normal world of cause and effect, the connection disappears. So the answer to our question is really another question: not 'What time is it', but '*Which* time is it? What is the dynamic *quality* of the time? How does this particular kind of time *change* things for *me*?' These are the sorts of question oracles can answer.

THE SPIRIT OF THE TIME

The *I Ching* is the oldest divinatory oracle to survive the 'disenchantment of the world'. Each of the book's 64 Figures acts as a mirror for the unconscious forces shaping a given problem or situation. They are an invitation to a dialogue with the 'spirit of the time' and begin a creative process that adjusts the balance between you, the questioner, and the energies or forces behind your situation. It can warn you, encourage you, describe possible outcomes or reveal hidden dangers.

In traditional terms, the *I Ching* 'provides symbols' which 'comprehend the light of the gods'. It produces an echo that 'reaches the depths, grasps the seeds and penetrates the wills of all beings under heaven'. It can discern the seeds of future developments and move the dark psychological places where we are caught or 'hung up'.

The Way of Change

The *I Ching* does this because it is more than a book and an oracle. It is a 'way', a tool we can use on our spiritual journey through life. It continually opens a path that we can follow. Through its symbols and the connection with the spirit they provide, it enables its users to 'follow the order of their own nature and of fate'. It opens a dialogue with a deep inner voice that seeks to keep us connected to the living world, the 'on-going process of the real'.

WORDS THAT HELP
YOU FIND THE PATH

Tao or way

The *I Ching* uses certain key words to indicate this path and how it works. The first is *tao* or 'way'. *Tao* permeates, supports, moves and changes everything in our world, seen and unseen. The word itself means 'way' or 'path', and is made up of the graphs (symbolic drawings) for 'head' or 'first' and 'walk' – the first motion in the universe. It is the 'on-going process of the real', a great and mysterious flow of energy that animates, moves and shapes the world. It offers a way or path to each thing in this world, and gives it its potential identity.

To be 'in' *tao* is to experience meaning. It brings joy, connection, freedom, compassion, creativity and love. The two basic divinatory

signs used in the *I Ching* reflect this distinction. One term indicates
that *the way is open*, that an action or direction accords with *tao* and
thus releases good fortune and transformative energy. The other
term indicates that *the way is closed*, that an action or direction is not
in accord with *tao* and will cut you off from the spirit and leave you
open to danger.

The Two Fundamental Powers

The *tao* or way articulates as two basic qualities. These two qualities
reflect dark and light, moon and sun, water and fire, soft and hard,
dissolution and creation, love and hate, dream and waking, death
and life, female and male. The people who made the *I Ching* 'saw'
each thing as a particular mixture of these qualities and could thus
predict the way they would move and develop. The oldest words for
these qualities are the terms *great* and *small*, or *strong* and *supple*. They
later became known as *yin* and *yang*.

These words describe ways to orient your will. They indicate
the most basic thing you can do to be in accord with the spirit of
the time.

YANG POWER OR BEING GREAT

Certain times and situations call upon you to be *Great* and *strong*, to
collect your strength, have an idea, impose your will and act. The
Great person is someone who has done this consistently and has thus
acquired power and influence. This orientation represents the influence of the *Great* in someone's life.

YIN POWER OR BEING SMALL

Other times and situations demand that you be *Small* and *supple*,
that you let go of your importance and adapt to whatever crosses
your path. *Small people* can adjust to whatever happens in a flexible
and spontaneous way because they are not impeded by a sense of
self-importance. This represents the influence of the *Small* in someone's life.

ACCUMULATING *TE* OR POWER AND VIRTUE

By voluntarily adjusting your will to the time, and seeing the spirit-
value in the events of life, you accumulate a special *power and virtue*
called *Te*, which comes from following the way. This *power and
virtue*, which can directly influence others, enables you to become
who you are intrinsically meant to be: a true individual or accomplished person.

THE REALIZING PERSON

Someone who follows the *tao* or *way* and uses the Change to
accumulate *power and virtue* is called a *realizing person*, a 'child of

the leader' or most important thing. This person is on the way to becoming realized or accomplished through contact with the spirit of change. She or he uses the oracle to help in this endeavour.

HEAVEN AND EARTH

The *I Ching* portrays a dynamic yet timeless world. This world grew out of the landscape of northern China: plains, rivers, valleys, the wide earth stretching to a mountainous horizon, the arching sky full of tumbling clouds and sudden storms. There are farms, fields and simple huts, villages, fortified cities surrounded by circles of dwellings, magnificent royal palaces and tombs, all separated by forest, mountains and wide tumultuous rivers. The wilderness between things is full of unexpected encounters and mystic retreats. Wandering groups of nomads and herdsmen roam the borders.

This is a place where a wide variety of people live and work. We can see peasants, nomads, merchants, nobles, kings, husbands and wives, courtesans, slaves, children, wanderers and soldiers as they eat and drink, love and hate, work, hope and scheme, make war and peace, despair or find enlightenment, face disaster or are full of joy.

This beautiful and constantly changing world was called *Heaven and Earth*. It was sometimes seen as a great turtle, swimming through the fertile seas of chaos that surround us. Heaven and Earth was filled with the Myriad Beings, the 10,000 things, all going their individual ways, each linked to Heaven and Earth which nourishes and sustains them.

The Souls and Spirits
Heaven and Earth is full of other beings, too, the *Souls and Spirits*. These are gods, demons, angry ghosts, ancestors and nature spirits, many of whom can enlighten, guide and give power to human intelligence. The landscape is dotted with points of close encounter with these beings: field altars, shrines, towers, grave mounds and temples of all kinds.

Living in *tao*
These spirits are messengers – they who announce how Heaven and Earth is moving, and who participate in its power. Any action, even just living and enjoying your life, only has a real chance of success if it connects with the spirits. What we now call meaning, or a meaningful experience, is just such a connection. The people who lived in Heaven and Earth would have called it being or living in *tao*.

Making the Symbols

According to tradition, the Ancient Sages, the diviners and shamans, made *symbols* of all these mysteries. The Sages *symbolized* the world for all people through a kind of shamanic clear-seeing or deep imaginative induction. So everything in it became a connection to the potent world of the spirit. These symbols became the writing of the *I Ching*.

THE WORLD OF SYMBOLS
AND THE FLOW OF TIME

Personal Time and Unconscious Time

These symbols are a manifestation of the power and virtue that pervades the spirit world. They are connected with a particular kind of time. We usually think of time as flowing from the past into the future. We *were* born, we *are* living, we *will* die. This is personal time. The world of symbols is connected with a different stream of time. It flows from the future through the present into the past. The *I Ching* describes this in the words 'coming' and 'going'. Symbols (and the events they describe) *come* from the future, casting their shadows in front of them. Then they *go* away from you and flow into the past.

'Seeing' What is Coming

The symbols that move on this stream are 'seeds of time' that represent the future. The *I Ching* can give us access to this flow of symbolic or 'unconscious' time. By 'turning around', so to speak, and seeing symbolically, we can see the probable form things will take. Since our troubles very often come from clinging to what is present, this helps us to let go and open a space for what will soon enter our lives.

The Shapes of Time

The many ancient sages and diviners who made the *I Ching*, 'symbolized' anything they saw that had spirit power, that reflected the seeds of time. This means that the actions and objects of the *I Ching* are not merely historical artefacts, but *shapes of time*. This world of symbols offers us a unique and comprehensive model of the human imagination and the forces that move it. Because these symbols tell us about the shape of our deep imagination, they describe the flow of time now as effectively as they did 3,000 years ago.

INVISIBLE BEINGS AND SPIRIT

The *I Ching* takes for granted that humans live in a world that is alive. It is a 'magical' world in which we participate through words and images. This world has a purpose that directly affects us. We share this world with many kinds of invisible beings; they are part of us, in that they affect our feelings and behaviour, but they come and go as they please. We cannot control them.

The *I Ching* has a special set of ideas to deal with these spirits. It describes the actions of the various parts of our unconscious that influence us but of which we are not normally aware.

Spirits and Symbols

The first idea is that everything has a voice and can be a symbol that shows where the spirit world and the normal world intersect. We see this happening every night in our dreams. If you remember your dreams, then watch what happens the following day, you will see this symbolizing at work quite clearly.

Spirits and Energy

The second idea is that the spirit world is a kind of energy, a powerful energy that helps shape the world we experience. This energy shows itself in many ways, which are reflected in the many kinds of imaginary beings. But the primary thing is the connection. One of the most significant divinatory signs in the *I Ching* is: *there is a connection to the spirits.* This means that spirit or energy is flowing into you. You can count on deep sources of power and guidance within you to help you through. This is a sign of truth, sincerity and trust; humanity's higher powers.

Shen or Helping Spirits

The *shen* are 'high' spirits that can aid humans. They are a kind of bright spirit or deep intuitive clarity that characterizes a 'realized' human being. Sages may be said to have a shen or helping spirit. The old shamans spoke of 'cleaning the house of the soul' so the shen would come to live there. Later, philosophers saw them as embodying moral and intellectual power and integrity. They confer power and depth on the heart and mind. Someone who develops one of these 'bright spirits' can see the causes and the courses of things and knows what to do about them. The *I Ching* was particularly used to follow or duplicate this old shamanic path. It helps you contact the spirit and, over time, to find this spirit-voice within yourself. It gives your guardian angel, deep self or guiding spirit an actual voice in your life.

Adversity: the Angry Ghost

Another kind of spirit often encountered is described through the word *adversity*. In this world, part of each human remains with the earth and the tomb after death. When this soul is angered through neglect, when it has committed a great crime or suffered a great injury, it returns to inflict suffering on the living. This suffering is often a plague, an epidemic or a highly contagious kind of psychological disorder. This closely parallels the way we repress memories, feelings and experiences and have them return to haunt us. These memories can pass from person to person, and from generation to generation. This *adversity*, present danger with its roots in the past, is symbolized as an angry ghost. The danger, be it anger, injustice or hidden corruption, must be confronted, exorcized or pacified.

Ancestors

One further aspect of this spirit world is the ancestors. Even today, each Chinese house has its ancestor tablets and shrine. Each village had an ancestral hall. The land was once dotted with hilltop shrines and grave mounds. The image of the ancestors offered an immediate connection to the spirit world. You went to the grave mound or shrine not just to offer sacrifice, but to ponder and ask guidance. The image of the ancestors opened the door to the power and wisdom of the unconscious world.

THE NAME OF THE BOOK

The most important 'spirit', however, is contained in the name of the book itself: *I* (pronounced 'ee'). The book really has three names. *I Ching*, the most familiar in the West, means 'Classic of *I*'. This comes from the time when five 'classic' books were established in China, around 200 BCE. The older name is *Chou I*, or 'The *I* Book of the Kings of Chou', who were the first to assemble and use it around 1100 BCE. Quite frequently it is simply called 'The *I*'.

This word is usually translated as 'change' or 'changes', but it is really more precise than that. The *I Ching* contains models of orderly change, such as the change of the seasons, the movement of the planets or the stages of life, and models of transformations like water becoming ice, or a caterpillar becoming a butterfly. What is called '*I*' really occurs *outside* these models of predictable change.

The first meaning of *I* is 'trouble'. It indicates sudden storms, loss, times when what is thought to be stable suddenly becomes fluid or vanishes. Structures break down; something extraordinary occurs.

The second meaning of *I* is the response to this kind of trouble: versatility, imaginative mobility, openness, something easy and light, not difficult and heavy. It suggests a fluid personal identity and a variety of imaginative stances. Through *I* you can change and move as fluidly and unpredictably as the creative force it describes. The *I* and its symbols describe the movements of the spirits that are the 'seeds of events' in the world. The spirits and their symbols connect the *I* of the universe to your own *I*, your creative imagination, if you choose to use them.

THE HISTORICAL DEVELOPMENT OF THE BOOK

The *Chou I*

The creation of the *Chou I*, the original name of the book, was associated with the rise of the Chou Kings and the fall of the previous Shang Dynasty. This is characterized in the book itself as a 'difficult time', full of sorrows. The eventual victory of the Chou nobles was thought to have restored the Golden Age to China. One of the most important tools in their struggle was their 'Book of *I*'.

By about 500 BCE the Chou kingdoms had fallen apart. It was during this time of civil unrest, the Warring States period, that the *individual* use of the oracle began. The book's purpose was transformed. It helped individuals find their way through the chaos of a crumbling social order.

The Classic of *I*

During the Han Dynasty (206 BCE – 220 CE), what was called the *Chou I* or 'Changes of Chou' became the *I Ching* or 'Classic of Change'. The Han was the first great Imperial state in China, and it gathered and standardized many things. The written language was codified and clarified and five canonical texts or 'Classics' were established. The first was the 'Classic of *I*', the *I Ching*. Imperial scholars edited the text and put it into the new form of writing. They also collected and wrote down the various oral 'traditions' or teachings about how the oracle was used. These became the 'Ten Wings' that were attached to the central text. One of them in particular, the *Hsi tzu chuan* or *Ta chuan*, the 'Commentary on the Attached Words' or 'Great Commentary', became one of the most important documents in Chinese culture. It explained how the world worked and how, through divination, we could find our proper place in it.

Confucianism

This version of the *I Ching* lasted well into the twentieth century. It was used and interpreted in many different ways, from popular to academic. A very influential system of interpretation grew up among the scholar-bureaucrats who served the government, a system called

Confucianism or Neo-Confucianism. This moral and philosophical system was based on a particular interpretation of the *tao*. Neo-Confucians said that *tao* was a set of hierarchical cosmic and social relations: just as heaven is above, and earth below, so man is above, woman below; the husband above, the wife below; the elder above, the younger below; the ruler above, the subject below; the yang power above, and the yin power below. These ideas of above and below were a judgement of value and intrinsic worth, a strict moral and social hierarchy. Internalizing this hierarchy was the Confucian idea of 'being in *tao*'. They developed an elaborate interpretation of the words and figures of the *I Ching* to support this hierarchical morality.

The Change Today

This century has brought a historic re-vision of the *I Ching*, taking the Neo-Confucian interpretation apart. Independent sources of the earliest types of written Chinese were discovered, and much light has been thrown upon divination practices and the meanings of words and phrases outside of their Confucian definitions. The identity of the book itself is once again changing. We can now recover its old oracular power and, at the same time, find a new place for it in the imagination of our time.

QUICK GUIDE:

Bridges to the World of Symbols

These reflections may help you enter into the spirit of the symbolic world of the *I Ching* and understand why people use it.

- The *I Ching* is an attempt to understand and work with the change that is always happening to us. It lets you participate in this process rather than be an unconscious victim.

- The *I Ching* can give you a mirror of the hidden forces at work in your unconscious, the psychological and spiritual forces acting behind the scenes in your life.

- The *I Ching* tells you about the *quality* of time, what this *particular moment* in time means to *you*. Thus it helps you to understand and follow 'the order of your own nature and of fate'.

- There are three important words that characterize the *I Ching* as an imaginative and spiritual practice: *tao* or *way*, *power and virtue* (*te*) and the *realizing person* (*chün tzu*). The *tao* is the fundamental *way* or flow of all things. To be 'in' *tao* is to experience meaning and joy. By doing this you accumulate the *power and virtue* to become who you really are meant to be. The *realizing person* is someone who uses the oracle to help in this process of self-realization.

- What we call the unconscious, the ancient world called the world of gods and spirits. These spirits are forces within us. They can help us by sending a flow of energy and inspiration, or they can hinder us by confronting us with negative emotions and bad memories. The divinatory signs of the *I Ching* indicate which kind of forces are at work in a given situation and how you can deal with them.

- The ancient creators of the *I Ching* made their entire world into symbols. They took specific events and 'saw' what was universal in them, what had '*spirit power*'. By doing this they gave us a living model of the human imagination. There are parts of our imagination or unconscious that act with a great deal of independence. We can use the symbols of the *I Ching* to put us in contact with these forces in order to understand what they are preparing to do.

- The *I Ching* and its symbols are associated with a particular kind of time. Usually we see time as flowing from the past through the present into the future. The symbols in the *I Ching* move in a stream of time that flows in the other direction, from the future through the present into the past. That is why they are called 'seeds of time'. They reflect future events that are moving towards us.

- The *I Ching* and its symbols preside over the birth and activity of the *helping spirit*, a deep inner guide who helps us shape our destiny. The symbols give you a way to talk to this inner guide.

- The word *I* (the name of the book) tells you how this works. *I* means both 'trouble' and the solution to trouble – imaginative change, mental mobility, connection to the creative unconscious. This spirit first manifests as a problem or difficulty that interferes with you and leads you to consult the oracle. Through using the symbols of the book to talk with this 'trouble', you turn it into a new and deeper spiritual clarity. This is 'talking to your self' in the deepest and most religious sense. It is a continual process of transformation.

Lines and Diagrams

The 64 Figures of the *I Ching* are made up of both words and diagrams. The diagrams organize the words and give you access to them. They also have a meaning of their own. The book is thus a combination of two kinds of thought, one that works with the meaning of images, and one that works with the meaning of geometric diagrams.

The Two Kinds of Line

There are two basic kinds of line used in the diagrams of the *I Ching*. These two kinds of line participate in the nature of the two fundamental powers that join to make the *tao* or way.

The Strong	**The Supple**
Action: firm, unyielding, moving, persisting, enduring, whole	*Structuring*: flexible, adaptable, still, yielding, pliant, opened

In their oldest form these two kinds of line were used as a 'yes–no' oracle. Versions of this kind of divination are in active use all over the world. The basic answer here, however, was not 'yes' or 'no', but related to what kind of attitude to take towards a problem: whether to take action, be aggressive and assert your will; or be yielding, stay in place and adapt to what comes.

Change and Transformation

It was also realized very early that these two powers were continually in motion. They were constantly waxing, waning and changing shape. They *changed* their nature slowly, one growing larger while the other grew smaller, then suddenly *transformed* themselves into one another. The diviners sought a way to reflect this, so they doubled the lines to show the powers in both a state of slow change and a state of sudden transformation into their opposites, as *young* and *old*.

Old or *transforming* yang energy	Young or *stable* yin energy	Old or *transforming* yin energy	Young or *stable* yang energy

The new lines enter the bottom of the Figure, and leave at the top. A 'stable' situation is always a *mixture* of the two powers. It is not static, but is gradually *changing*. One power slowly grows and *changes* until it totally controls the situation. At that point it suddenly *transforms* into its opposite and the slow growth begins again from the other side. These four configurations show two stable conditions of gradual change and two conditions of radical transformation, cracks in time where action occurs.

The Four-line Oracle

Consulted through marked sticks or dice in a number of ways (*see* pp 33–36), these four lines were a frequently used oracle, and have parallels throughout the world. They also gave birth to many different kinds of cycle, such as the four seasons, four directions, or four stages of life. In the *I Ching* the same four kinds of line became the basis of consultation. They are usually noted like this:

old yang	young yin	old yin	young yang
transforms into>		*transforms into>*	

THE SIX-LINE DIAGRAMS OR HEXAGRAMS

The next development represents one of those quantum leaps that so surprise us in human thought. In the history of divination, this is comparable to the discovery of the zero. Someone, somewhere, 'piled' six of these lines on top of one another to make a *gua*, a 'divinatory pile' that we now call a diagram or 'hexagram'. When you make all the possible combinations of six strong and supple lines, you get 64 diagrams. Because each line can transform itself into its opposite, all the diagrams can turn into each other in a continuous cycle. And, because each of the lines can be determined by chance, the 'spirit of the time' could directly choose which diagram was an accurate representation. The diagram or *gua* became itself a magic sign and could be used to invoke the power it signified. Together, these 64 diagrams provided the basis for a language with which the spirits could speak directly to humans.

Evolution of the Diagrams or Gua

These diagrams were used to display and give access to the tradition of words, omens, sayings and events that had been symbolized as the 'seeds of time'. Like scientists studying the model of a process that participates in the process itself, diviners studied and speculated about the diagrams. Each diagram was thought of as a 'slice of time' that characterized an archetypal 'moment' by showing how the two fundamental powers were interacting. Each was thought of as having six empty 'places', numbered from the bottom up. Energy flowed through these places, leaving a trail or track represented by the lines. Each diagram was given a name and a number and had divinatory formulae assigned to it. Special texts were given to each place or line. Thus the diagrams became Figures, combinations of words and lines that portrayed the Shapes of Change. Here is the basic 'empty' form of all the 64 Figures, with its six numbered places.

```
6 [                    ]
5 [                    ]
4 [                    ]

3 [                    ]
2 [                    ]
1 [                    ]
```

Number: _____
Name: _____

THE RELATING FIGURE

Once the diagrams became Figures with texts attached, the next important discovery was what is called the 'Relating Figure'. Diviners realized that when one or more of the lines *transform* they not only key a special text, they produce a second diagram. The *transforming* lines change into their opposite, while all the other lines remain the same, thus *transforming* the Figure as a whole. This gives *two* Figures, connected by the transforming lines. Here is an example:

```
6 [ ___ ]                              [ _____ ]
5 [ __x__ ]         transforms to>     [ _____ ]
4 [ _____ ]                          [ _____ ]

3 [ ___  ___ ]                         [ ___  ___ ]
2 [ ___  ___ ]                         [ ___  ___ ]
1 [ ___o___ ]       transforms to>     [ ___  ___ ]
```

Primary Figure   *transforms to:*   **Relating Figure**
Name: *51 Shake*   Name: *45 Clustering*

Primary Figure

This is the normal form of an *I Ching* reading. A figure is formed, through one of several methods, that usually has one or more *transforming* lines. This figure talks about the basic situation and how you can deal with it. When the transforming lines are changed they produce a second figure.

Relating Figure

The second figure represents how you are 'related' to the basic figure. It can be a future development. It can also point to a past event that brought you here, a warning, a goal, a particular attitude or a deep desire – whatever is 'relating' you to the basic answer. It is the 'sea' or ground feeling in which the basic figure swims.

THE FAMILY OF THREE-LINE DIAGRAMS OR TRIGRAMS

The division of the six-line diagram (*gua*, called 'hexagram') into two three-line diagrams (also *gua*, called 'trigram') was another very influential development. The eight trigrams or *pa gua*, the eight possible combinations of three strong and supple lines, became basic units of Chinese thought. They were used to describe the workings of the cosmos and to organize a wide range of other cycles and associations – directions, body parts, feelings, colours, seasons and actions. Even today the *pa gua* or Eight Figures are used as a charm or talisman to ward off evil influences and attract beneficial *ch'i* energy.

Names, Symbols and Actions

These three-line figures are not abstract. They have names, associations, specific *symbols* and *actions* that characterize them. They were thought of as spirits representing the basic energies at work in the natural and human worlds. They are major figures in the *I Ching*, so you should become acquainted with them.

Here are the eight trigrams with their associations, symbols and actions. They are given in what was called the order according to *Fu Hsi*, that is, in corresponding pairs that represent father and mother and three pairs of sons and daughters. This was also called the Pre-Heaven arrangement, for it represented a symmetrical, fixed cosmos that typified a changeless golden age.

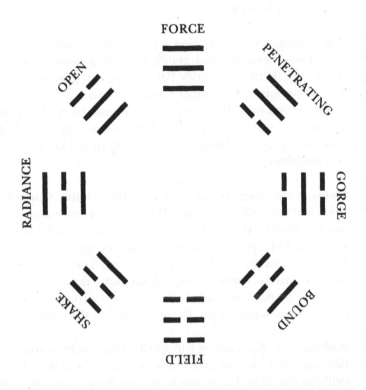

The order according to *Fu Hsi* or Pre-heaven arrangement

Force, CH'IEN: Force is a dragon, a creative spirit that lives in the waters and in the heavens. This spirit is a dynamic shape-changer. It can give you creative power and enduring strength. Its symbol is **heaven**; its action is to **persist**. It is made of only strong lines. In the family it is the father.

Field, K'UN: Field is the womb that gives birth to all things. This spirit nourishes everything; without it nothing could exist. It can give you the power to give shape to things, to make thoughts and images visible. Its symbol is **earth**; its action is to **yield**, serve and bring forth. It is made up of only supple lines. In the family it is the mother.

Shake, CHEN: Shake is the thunder spirit, who bursts forth from the earth below to arouse, excite and disturb. This spirit stirs things up and brings them out of hiding. It can arouse your energy and give you the strength to undertake difficult things. Its symbol is **thunder**; its action is to **rouse** or excite. It is made up of a stirring strong line below two dormant supple lines. In the family it is the first son.

Penetrating, SUN: Penetrating is the spirit of wood and wind. It is a subtle, beautiful and gentle spirit that permeates things and brings them to maturity. Penetrating can give you the ability to support and nourish things. It was associated with marriage and presides over the new house. Its symbol is **wind** and **wood**; its action is to **enter** from below. It is a supple line that nourishes two strong lines above it. In the family it is the first daughter.

Gorge, K'AN: Gorge is the spirit of rushing water. Gorge takes risks, like water falling, filling the holes in its path and flowing on. It dissolves things, carries them forward and cannot be stopped. This spirit can give you the energy to take risks, to focus your energy at a critical point, to confront and overcome obstructions. Its symbol is the **stream**, water flowing rapidly; its action is to **risk** and **fall**. It is the single strong line flowing between two supple lines. In the family it is the middle son.

Radiance, LI: Radiance is the spirit of fire, light, warmth and the magical power of awareness, a shape-changing bird with brilliant plumage that comes to rest on things. Radiance clings together with what it illuminates. It can give you the power to see and understand things, and to articulate ideas and goals. Its symbols are **brightness** and **fire**; its action is to hold or **cling together**. It is the single supple line that holds two strong lines together. In the family it is the middle daughter.

Bound, KEN: Bound is the mountain spirit, who limits and brings things to a close. This spirit suggests the Palace of the Immortals, the eternal images that end and begin all things. It can give you the power to articulate what you have gone through and make your accomplishments clear. Its symbol is the **mountain**; its action is to **still** or **stop** motion. It is the single strong line that stops two supple lines beneath it. In the family it is the youngest son.

Open, TUI: Open is the spirit of open water, the vapours that rise from lakes, ponds and marshes that fertilize and enrich. The friendliest and most joyous of spirits, Open brings stimulating words, profitable exchange, cheerful interaction, freedom from constraint. It can give you persuasive and inspiring speech, the ability to rouse things to action and create good feeling. Its symbol is the **mists**; its action is to **stimulate**. It is the single supple line that leads two strong lines forward.

In the family it is the youngest daughter.

The Later Heaven Arrangement and the Universal Compass

The trigrams were also organized according to the cyclic way they worked in the world of 'Later Heaven', the complicated world we live in now. This arrangement, also called the arrangement according to *King Wen*, was superimposed on a diagram of the eight directions to create a 'Universal Compass' with a virtually infinite variety of qualities associated along its axes. Any one of these qualities connected with all the others on the same axis. The whole group could then be connected to the divinatory system of the *I Ching* through one of the eight trigrams. Further, you could follow a cyclic progression of these times and qualities around the circumference of the circle in either direction to see what each quality would produce or destroy. Systems such as this are used throughout traditional science and medicine.

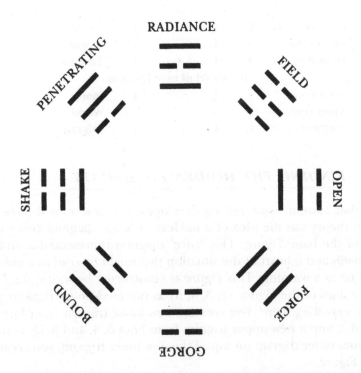

The order according to *King Wen* or Later Heaven arrangement

OUTER AND INNER WORLDS

The most interesting thing for us, however, is the idea that the upper and lower trigrams came to represent the interlocking activities of the *Outer and Inner Worlds*.

Each trigram has an individual symbol and action that typify it. The Figures or diagrams can be seen as being made up of two of these trigrams. If the lower is taken as the 'inner world' and the upper is taken as the 'outer world', then the Figure as a whole portrays the dynamic interconnection between the world of events and the world of the psyche. This view was further elaborated to suggest meanings for the various line positions based on their place in the 'inner' or 'outer' world. The first and sixth lines were seen as the entrance and the exit from the situation, with things moving from inside to outside. The second and fifth lines were seen as the centres of the inner and outer worlds, and the third and fourth lines described the transition between them.

exit	6	[ ]	**Outer**
outer centre	5	[ ]	**World**
transition	4	[ ]	**Trigram**
		threshold of manifestation	
transition	3	[ ]	**Inner**
inner centre	2	[ ]	**World**
entrance	1	[ ]	**Trigram**

FINDING THE HIDDEN POSSIBILITY

Another extremely interesting development that stemmed from trigram theory was the idea of a nuclear or 'core' diagram concealed within the basic Figure. This 'core' diagram represented a *Hidden Possibility* at the heart of the situation that might be read as a hidden goal or as a warning. This Figure is constructed by seeing the four inner lines of the Figure (2, 3, 4, 5) as two *overlapping* trigrams and then *unpacking* them. You create a new lower trigram from lines 2, 3 and 4, and a new upper trigram from lines 3, 4, and 5. By putting the new outer trigram on top of the new inner trigram, you create a new Figure.

		6 [ ]			
		5 [ ]		6	**Outer**
Inner	3	4 [ ]		5	**Nuclear**
Nuclear	2	3 [ ]		4	**Trigram**
Trigram	1	2 [ ]			
		1 [ ]			

The Nuclear Figure of *40 Loosening*, for example, would be *63 Already Fording*:

[—— ——]		6 [—— ——]
[—— ——] 6		5 [—————]
3 [—————] 5		4 [—— ——]
2 [—— ——] 4		3 [—————]
1 [—————]		2 [—— ——]
[—— ——]		1 [—————]

40 Loosening	**63 Already Fording**

The Family of Nuclear Figures

This discovery revealed an interesting facet of the deep structure of the 64 Figures. Each group of four Figures shares a common nuclear diagram; thus there are only 16 possible 'first generation' nuclear Figures. If you determine the nuclear diagram of these 16, you find they share four 'second generation' nuclear diagrams. These four are the first two Figures of the book, *1 Force* and *2 Field*, which represent the primal forces in the cosmos, and the last two Figures, *63 Already Fording* and *64 Not Yet Fording*, which show an action about to begin and one already under way. These four figures are unique. The first two are their own nuclear diagrams; the last two are each other's nuclear diagram. Thus a chart of all 64 Figures can be made and the line of action for any situation traced back through the series of nuclear diagrams to these four basic sources. You can follow this line back when you work with a Figure to give you a sense of the hidden springs and direction of the action. In the chart on page 25, each nuclear Figure has a phrase attached to it that suggests its meaning.

THE OPPOSING FIGURE

If the Hidden Possibility or core diagram gives you a sense of what may be hidden at the centre of your Figure, the Opposing Diagram tells you what it is not. It gives you an image of the complete contrary, in order to help you focus more clearly on what the quality in question really is. Based on yin-yang theory, the Opposing Diagram is formed by substituting a yang line for every yin line, and a yin line for every yang line. Transforming lines are not taken into account. If we take the figure *40 Loosening*, for example, and change each line into its opposite, we would get the following:

```
6 [ ___  ___ ]              [ _____ ]
5 [ ___  ___ ]              [ _____ ]
4 [ _____ ]             [ ___  ___ ]


3 [ ___  ___ ]             [ _____ ]
2 [ _____ ]             [ ___  ___ ]
1 [ ___  ___ ]             [ _____ ]
```

Basic Figure	**Opposing Figure**
Name: *40 Loosening*	Name: *37 Dwelling People*

Here we see that *loosening* and setting things free from restraint and tension is the complete opposite of the family structure that holds *people* together in a *dwelling*. One holds things in and protects them; the other sets things free, breaks down structures and releases new energy.

THE STEPS OF CHANGE

Another way of using the diagrams is directly associated with the *transforming lines*. It is of particular help in a complex situation, where more than one line is transforming and a series of actions is shown. Each diagram consists of six lines. Each time *one* of these lines changes, it generates a particular Relating Figure. That means that each figure has a family of six other figures that are *related to it by the change of one single line*. When you have a reading with more than one transforming line, you can generate the Relating Figures associated with the change of each particular line. This gives you an idea of the *steps* or stages the change may pass through.

Here is an example. If you are working with *40 Loosening*, with three transforming lines (2, 4 and 5) that change it to *8 Grouping*, the diagrams would look like this:

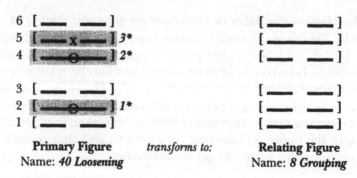

```
6 [ ___  ___ ]              [ ___  ___ ]
5 [ ___ x ___ ] 3*          [ _____ ]
4 [ ___ o ___ ] 2*          [ ___  ___ ]


3 [ ___  ___ ]              [ ___  ___ ]
2 [ ___ o ___ ] 1*          [ ___  ___ ]
1 [ ___  ___ ]              [ ___  ___ ]
```

Primary Figure	*transforms to:*	**Relating Figure**
Name: *40 Loosening*		Name: *8 Grouping*

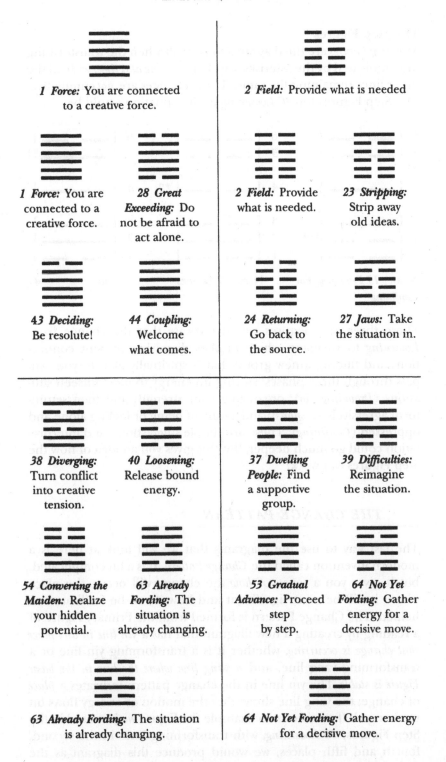

1 *Force:* You are connected to a creative force.

2 *Field:* Provide what is needed

1 *Force:* You are connected to a creative force.

28 *Great Exceeding:* Do not be afraid to act alone.

2 *Field:* Provide what is needed.

23 *Stripping:* Strip away old ideas.

43 *Deciding:* Be resolute!

44 *Coupling:* Welcome what comes.

24 *Returning:* Go back to the source.

27 *Jaws:* Take the situation in.

38 *Diverging:* Turn conflict into creative tension.

40 *Loosening:* Release bound energy.

37 *Dwelling People:* Find a supportive group.

39 *Difficulties:* Reimagine the situation.

54 *Converting the Maiden:* Realize your hidden potential.

63 *Already Fording:* The situation is already changing.

53 *Gradual Advance:* Proceed step by step.

64 *Not Yet Fording:* Gather energy for a decisive move.

63 *Already Fording:* The situation is already changing.

64 *Not Yet Fording:* Gather energy for a decisive move.

The Groups of Nuclear Figures or Hidden Possibilities

The Step Figures

The *Step Figures* are the diagrams that result when the transforming lines indicated by the asterisks are changed *one at a time*, with all the other lines remaining the same. These changes are *not* cumulative. The Step Figures for *40 Loosening* in this situation would be:

```
6 [ ___   ___ ]      6 [ ___   ___ ]      6 [ ___   ___ ]
5 [ ___   ___ ]      5 [ ___   ___ ]      5 [ _____ ]
*3                    
4 [ _____ ]      4 [ ___   ___ ] *2   4 [ _____ ]

3 [ _____ ]      3 [ ___   ___ ]      3 [ ___   ___ ]
2 [ ___   ___ ] *1   2 [ _____ ]      2 [ _____ ]
1 [ ___   ___ ]      1 [ ___   ___ ]      1 [ ___   ___ ]
```

Name: *17 Providing For*   Name: *7 Legions*   Name: 47
Confining

These three Step Figures would indicate that the change from *Loosening* to *Grouping*, which implies dissolving present connections and finding a new group that is spiritually akin to you, will pass through three phases: storing up energy to meet unseen situations (*Providing For*); organizing your strength and then setting forth agressively (*Legions*); and a time of being or feeling alone and oppressed (*Confining*). These are simple suggestions, and interpretation could go much deeper, but this gives you an idea of how the Step Figures can work.

THE CHANGE PATTERN

The last way to use the diagrams that we will look at here is a modern invention called the *Change Pattern*. It is a bit complicated, but it gives you a sense of *how* the change will occur, the place where it will be most significant and how it can be facilitated or helped. The Change Pattern is formed from the Primary Figure of a reading by creating a new diagram that has a *yin line in any place that change is occurring*, whether it is a transforming yin line or a transforming yang line, and *a yang line where the line in the basic Figure is stable*. The yin line in the change pattern indicates a *place of change*; the yang line shows that the motion or energy flows on unchanged. If we take as an example the Figure we just used in the Step Figures, *40 Loosening*, with transforming lines in the second, fourth and fifth places, we would produce this diagram as the Change Pattern:

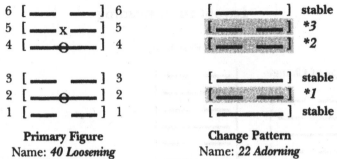

	Primary Figure		Change Pattern
	Name: *40 Loosening*		Name: *22 Adorning*

22 Adorning is about beautifying the appearance, making a show of elegance and bravery so that the exterior reflects inner changes. As a Change Pattern it would ask us to look at ways the changes going on can be made visible and beautiful. It indicates that elegance and beauty have a definite place in the situation and may act as a vehicle for the transformation.

A COMPLETE READING LAYOUT

The lines and diagrams we have looked at here give you a basis for understanding how the *I Ching* organizes and displays its words and symbols. They provide the means to get an answer and help to describe the quality of time, the 'moment' that connects you to the spirit and the way. In the section 'Consulting the Oracle' (pp 31–7) you will learn how to produce your initial six lines.

We can lay out all of these possibilities into a plan for a complete reading. It can show you the more subtle relations in an answer and help you locate the 'voice' of the oracle more precisely. But do not think you have to learn all of these in one day, or that all of them will always be interesting. They are perspectives and tools to help you. They will become easier to recognize as you become more familiar with the names and shapes of the Figures. The fundamental reading is a Primary Figure with one or more *transforming lines* that turns into a second Relating Figure. If there are no transforming lines in your reading, it simply indicates that the means of change is not yet ready to manifest itself. The situation will endure for a while.

Layout for a Reading

Hidden Possibility

Steps of Change

[____ ____]

③

47 Confining

          [____ ____]
          [_____]
          [_____]
          [____ ____]
          [_____]
          [____ ____]

63 Already Fording

6 [____ ____] **Outer**   [____ ____]
5 [___X___] **Trigram** [_____]
4 [___O___]   [_____]

3 [____ ____] **Inner**   [_____]
2 [___O___] **Trigram** [____ ____]
1 [_____]   [____ ____]

②

7 Legions

Primary Figure
40 Loosening

Relating Figure
8 Grouping

①

17 Providing For

Opposing Figure
37 Dwelling People

Change Pattern
22 Adorning

———O———	——— ———	———X———	———————
old yang	**young yin**	**old yin**	**young yang**
transforms into>	slowly changes into>	*transforms into>*	slowly changes into>

The Four Kinds of Line for the Primary Figure

SUMMARY:

Understanding the Lines and Diagrams

Here is a brief resumé of the kinds of line and how they are put together into the three- and six-line figures.

- There are four kinds of line used to make the diagrams: stable yin line and stable yang lines, *transforming* yin lines and *transforming* yang lines. In consulting the oracle the six lines of a Figure are generated by a method using chance (*see* pp 32–6).

—————O—————	——— ———	————X———	—————————
old yang	**young yin**	**old yin**	**young yang**
transforms into>		*transforms into>*	

- These lines may be used to build 64 different six-line diagrams and eight different three-line diagrams. Each has a name and a meaning. The six-line diagrams are seen as being made up of two three- line diagrams, one below or 'inside', and one above or 'outside'.

- Each diagram (or Figure, which is a diagram with the words in place) can change into any of the other Figures through the *transforming lines*. The usual answer to a question is a Primary Figure with at least one *transforming line* that changes it into a second or Relating Figure.

```
6 [          ]              [          ]
5 [          ]              [          ]
4 [          ]              [          ]

3 [          ]              [          ]
2 [          ]              [          ]
1 [          ]              [          ]
```

Primary Figure   *transforms to:*   **Relating Figure**

- Hidden inside each Figure is a core diagram or *Hidden Possibility*. It is formed by 'unpacking' the four *central* lines into two three-line figures, and setting the upper on top of the lower.

		6 [ ]		
		5 [ ]	6	Outer
Inner	3	4 [ ]	5	Nuclear
Nuclear	2	3 [ ]	4	Trigram
Trigram	1	2 [ ]		
		1 [ ]		

- By changing the yin lines into yang lines and vice versa in a Figure, you can generate the Opposing Figure, which gives you the opposite meaning to the Figure in question.

- In a Figure with several transforming lines, you can find the Steps of Change by transforming one line at a time. The resulting Figures show you the steps the change will pass through.

- You can find the Change Pattern by creating a Figure with a yin line for every transforming line in the original and a yang line for every stable line. This tells you about the means or area that the change will use.

- By examining the action of the upper or *outer* trigram and the *inner* or lower trigram you can read the interaction between the *Outer and Inner Worlds* in your situation.

Consulting the Oracle

A question is your real passport into the world of change, for it begins the creative process of talking with the oracle. The basic experience of using the *I Ching* is a feeling of being seen and valued. It reflects what the ancient world called the 'friendship of the spirit'.

A Chinese philosopher once remarked that all the different words used to talk about *tao* – spirit, fate, nature, way, pattern, the great ultimate – are really the same. They differ only according to how they are used: 'When it is above, you call it the way; when it is below, you call it an instrument; when you can see it, you call it a model; when you can hold it, you call it a tool'.

The Helping Spirit

The helping spirit is the *tao* or *way* acting as the guiding force of each individual being. It is our 'unconscious spirit' or guardian angel. It helps us shape our destiny and connects us with the way. It is very difficult for these spirits to talk directly to humans, as they do not have human language. The words of the oracle give your helping spirit a way to speak with you.

What Crosses You

This spirit will first manifest as a problem or difficulty. It is what 'crosses' you, what interferes with your conscious will. This problem is exactly where change is going to occur. It points at a 'critical moment', an opportunity to communicate and deepen your awareness.

You experience this as a disturbance, an unrest in your soul. Anxiety, confusion, a sense of being pulled in different directions, something hidden yet present, a need to know or see more, desire, repulsion or fear, the feeling you are grappling with something that cannot really be dealt with through rational means; all these indicate that there is an unknown force at work within you. The words of the oracle are meant to open communication with this force. By giving voice to the helping spirit, they can move the soul from where it is 'caught' or 'hung up' and re-establish the flow of the way.

FINDING THE RIGHT QUESTION

The first step is to present the problem as a question. Take some time with it. The clearer the question, and the deeper your perception of the issues around it, the more precise the oracle's answer will be.

Soul-searching

Basically, making a question has two parts. The first is 'soul-searching'. Search out the feelings, images, experiences, tensions, issues and connections that surround your problem. Articulate what you feel and think, what is at stake for you, any relevant memories, dreams, fears, anxieties, desires. You do not have to put all this together to 'make sense'. Just try to see what is there, no matter how contradictory. Talking with someone else can often be of great help in bringing these things out.

Make the Question Clear

The second step is to formulate a clear question. If possible, base this on what you *want* to do. Be as precise and honest as you can about your desire. Ask 'What about doing ... ?' or 'What would happen if I ... ?' An alternative is to ask for an imaginative stance towards an issue: 'What should my attitude towards ... be?' If you are confused about something, you can ask for an image. If you simply do not understand what is going on, ask for orientation: 'What is happening?' In any event, the oracle will offer an image – in words and figures – that is meant to connect you with the hidden forces at work in the situation as a whole. It will work with and through the material you have brought out, though often it offers a quite new perspective.

There are other ways to ask questions. The Chinese used the book as one of both wisdom and strategy. Thus, if you have a project or plan that you feel is worthwhile, you can ask 'How can I best achieve ... ?' The answer will give you an orientation towards the goal or, perhaps, a warning about its wisdom. If you are facing a set of alternatives, you may ask for an image of both possibilities: 'What about doing A? What about doing B?' Because the ideal of the *way* and the person who wishes to follow it is built into the book, it cannot be used for evil or manipulative ends. By asking a manipulative question, you can cut off communication with the oracle, possibly permanently.

Believing or Experiencing?

The question is your point of entrance into the world of change. Remember, there is real spirit at work in all this, a force that, though friendly, should be treated with respect. It reaches out to you with an offer of help. 'Personifying' a book in this way is a difficult concept for modern Western people, but it is not really a matter of belief, more one of imagination and experience. At this point all you need is an open mind and a certain basic respect. If the dialogue continues over time, you may come to know and love this voice of change.

GIVING CHANCE A CHANCE

Divination is a universal part of human culture, and has been used for centuries. Its symbols and signs are still relied on by many people throughout the world. There are certain elements that are common to almost all these divinatory procedures. First, there is an inquirer, a human being with a question or problem. Second, there is some kind of listener, a god, spirit, intelligence or unconscious force not bound by the normal rules of time and space. Third, there is a symbolic language through which the listener can speak. And, uniting them all, is chance.

Flip a coin, draw straws, pick a number; the die is cast, it's written in the stars, don't tempt fate, my lucky number – these expressions reveal the shattered remnants of a much older sense of 'chance' than our current idea of 'meaningless coincidence'. Old Chinese, for example, has no word for the modern kind of chance. 'Chance' is either spontaneous action, meaningful coincidence or the influence of an unseen force. In divination, it is the vehicle of your helping spirit, the way you are connected to the cosmos.

Chance and Fate

As in most divination systems, to get an answer from the *I Ching* you must rely on chance or random selection. You separate and count out a pile of yarrow stalks, throw coins, sticks or dice, pick out various coloured marbles or grains of rice. All these procedures rely on chance as something *beyond your conscious control* in order to produce the symbol that answers your question. The *spirit of the time* does the choosing, empowered by the focus of your question and the symbolic language available to it. A 'magical' explanation of this would say that the instruments used in the choice *participate* in the nature of the cosmic process; they are 'unconscious mirrors of spirit'. A more modern idea is that the symbols of the *I Ching* are living records of what we call *synchronous* occurrences, things that occur together and create meaning without a rational cause. Your question and the symbol system of the oracle set up a field of potential meaning. The chance selection of numbers and lines participates in and *re-creates* the synchronicity of the event. The entrance of chance into the field of meaning *participates* in the nature of fate. It connects the individual and the world of symbols.

The word *fate* as it is used in the *I Ching* is very interesting. It means both the *limits* of life, such as birth, death and momentous occurrences, and a *mandate*, a charge or responsibility given to you by your destiny. The oracle turns what seems to be a limit or dead-lock into an assignment from the spirit. Chance is the crack through which this transformation can appear.

ACCESSING THE CHANGE

The six-line Figures of the *I Ching* are the link between your question and the oracle's answer. To find your answer you must produce six lines, counting from the bottom to the top. These lines must be produced by chance.

There are several ways to produce these six lines. Some people have used four-sided sticks, with each side representing one of the four kinds of line, or two-sided slats of bamboo, shells or roots with the sides representing yin or yang. The oldest method counts out 49 yarrow stalks. The newest systems generate the figures with a computer.

Prepare Yourself

Before using any of these methods, search out your question and write it down. Set off a space where you can be peaceful and undisturbed. Open your inner concentration. Repeat your question to yourself, but do not focus on an answer. Let your mind relax, then make the divination, using whichever method you have chosen. Keep a note of anything that 'pops up' during the procedure. Note down the numbers or lines from the bottom up. If any are changing, generate the Relating Figure. Then turn to the *Key to the Hexagrams* and, by using the lower and upper trigrams, locate the number and the name of your answer. It is a very good idea to record your consultations with the date, question and answer, and comments about anything that particularly struck you.

The Coin Method

One of the most widespread kinds of 'tossing' oracle is the coin oracle. This was popularized in the Southern Sung period (1127–1279) and has been used for several hundred years. You must have three similar coins, and old Chinese bronze coins with square holes in the middle are often used. Heads (the side with four characters) are yang and are given the value 3. Tails (the side with either two or no characters) are yin and are given the value 2. You throw the three coins six times and add the numbers they represent each time. The total will always be 6, 7, 8 or 9. Record the kind of line each number refers to (6 = transforming yin; 7 = stable yang; 8 = stable yin; 9 = transforming yang).

9	8	6	7
——O——	—— ——	——x——	————
old yang	young yin	old yin	young yang
transforms into>		*transforms into>*	

Form your figure from the bottom up, then form the Relating Figure if there are any transforming lines. Use the *Key to the Hexagrams* to determine the numbers and names.

The Yarrow Stalk Method

The coin oracle yields quick results, but it does not penetrate as deeply into a situation as the older yarrow stalk oracle. Like all methods that use dice or toss sticks, the odds in the coin method are symmetrical. This reflects a binary 'either-or' choice between yin and yang that is not really accurate. Yin and yang are *asymmetrical* in their *qualities*, and it is this asymmetry that keeps our world in motion. The odds in the yarrow stalk oracle directly reflect the tendency of yin energy to stay in place, and that of yang energy to move.

To use the more ceremonial yarrow stalk oracle, you need a set of 50 thin sticks about 12–16 inches long, traditionally stalks of yarrow or *achillea millefolium*, taken from the tips of the plants. The basic unit of this process is dividing and counting out the bunch of yarrow stalks three times. Each time this is done it produces a number, and thus a line of your figure. Again, remember you are working from the bottom up.

- Put the bunch of 50 yarrow stalks on the table in front of you. Take one stalk and put it aside. This is the Observer or Witness. It will remain unused *throughout the entire process of forming a Figure.*
- Divide the remaining bunch into two random portions.
- Take one stalk from the pile on your left. Put it between the fourth and fifth fingers of your left hand.
- Count out the pile on the right into groups of four, laying out the groups clearly on the table in front of you. Pick it up in your left hand and count it out with your right. Count out the sticks until you have a remainder of 4, 3, 2, or 1. You must have a remainder.
- Put this remainder between the third and fourth fingers of your left hand.
- Take the remaining pile and count it out in groups of four, until you have a remainder of 4, 3, 2 or 1. Lay out the groups clearly on the table in front of you. Put the remainder between the second and third fingers of your left hand.

- Take all the stalks which you have put between your fingers and lay them aside. They are out *for this round.*
- Make one bunch of the stalks that remain and repeat the procedure. Again, lay the stalks you have put between your fingers aside at the end of the process.
- Repeat the process a third time. This time, count the number of groups of four left on the table in front of you. This number should be 6, 7, 8 or 9. It indicates the first or *bottom* line of your figure.
- To get the complete figure, repeat this process five more times, building the figure from the bottom up. When you finish, gather the stalks and return them to their container or wrapping. Then use the *Key to the Hexagrams* (*see* pp 186–7) to find the names and the numbers.

The Marble Method

The coins and the yarrow stalks are the most frequently used traditional methods. The coins are quick, but the odds aren't accurate. The yarrow stalks are more effective, and more beautiful, but the procedure is complicated and time-consuming.

A new way was invented recently that combines the two. It is as simple and direct as the coins, but has the same mathematical odds as the yarrow stalks. You need a small bowl and a total of 16 marbles of four different colours: *one* of one colour, *three* of the second colour, *five* of the third colour and *seven* of the fourth colour. Your choice of colours is completely arbitrary, but make sure you remember which colour is which.

In this method, each colour represents a different kind of line. Put all sixteen into the bowl. The one marble of the first colour represents the least frequent line, a yin line changing into a yang line (1 out of 16 chances). The three marbles of the second colour represent yang lines changing into yin lines (3 out of 16 chances). The five marbles of the third colour represent stable yang lines (5 out of 16 chances). The seven marbles of the fourth colour represent stable yin lines (7 out of 16 chances). These ratios reflect how yin energy likes to stay where it is, and how yang energy likes to move.

Now, shake and mix the marbles. Without looking, pick one from the bowl. Draw the kind of line this colour represents. Put the marble back into the bowl. Shake the bowl again and, without looking, pick out a second marble. Draw the kind of line this colour represents. Repeat until you have six lines, again counting from the bottom up. This is your Primary Figure. If there are any transforming lines, change them and create the Relating Figure. Then use the *Key to the Hexagrams* to determine numbers and names.

RECORDING YOUR ANSWERS

Here is a type of form to note your results from any of these methods. You can use it to go on to generate an entire layout (*see* pp 27–8).

6 [   ]   [   ]
5 [   ]   **Outer Trigram**   [   ]
4 [   ]   [   ]

3 [   ]   [   ]
2 [   ]   **Inner Trigram**   [   ]
1 [   ]   [   ]

Primary Figure   *transforms to:*   **Relating Figure**

Number: ____   Number: ____
Name: _____   Name: _____

SUMMARY:

A Quick Guide to Using the Oracle

- Make a clear question. The clearer the question, the clearer the answer will be. Decide exactly what this question *means* to you.

- Set off a quiet, calm place where you can pose the question and work with the answer.

- Using one of the methods described on pp 33–36, generate the six lines that make up one of the *Change*'s 64 divinatory figures.

- There are four possible types of line, as follows:

——O——	—— ——	——X——	————————
old yang (9)	young yin (8)	old yin (6)	young yang (7)
transforms into>		*transforms into>*	

- Record them starting from the bottom up. If there is a *transforming line*, change it in order to generate the Relating Figure.

```
6 [          ]              [            ]
5 [          ]              [            ]
4 [          ]              [            ]

3 [          ]              [            ]
2 [          ]              [            ]
1 [          ]              [            ]
```

Primary Figure   *transforms to:*   **Relating Figure**

Number: ____   Number: ____

Name: _____   Name: _____

- Use the *Key to the Hexagrams* on page 186 to identify the number and name of both of your figures.

- Read the basic texts of the Primary Figure and the special text attached to any line that is *transforming*. Then read the name and Image of the Relating Figure. You will probably feel an immediate intuitive connection. Keep that in mind as you explore all the possible ways the words could connect to your situation, 'turning and rolling them in your heart'.

Finding the Way

The *I Ching* acts primarily as a guide to making decisions. It can re-formulate your awareness of your situation, open up new connections and free your imagination. The idea is that through the consultation process we interact with the hidden forces creating our situation and discover how to respond most effectively. This creates 'bright spirit' or 'intuitive clarity' (*shen ming*).

Finding the mind of *tao*

You participate in this process by seeing your feelings, desires and concerns through the symbols of the oracle. By imagining yourself and your situation through these images you can re-direct the manner in which you are thinking about things. This is called 'finding the mind of *tao*'.

The *I Ching* was one of the foundations of Chinese culture, in the same way the Homeric epics or the Bible were foundations of much of Western culture. They are all, in the best sense of the word, myths or 'true fictions', shapes of the human spirit. There is, however, an important difference. Western mythology tells stories, full of heroes, gods and action. Chinese myths are *not* stories; they are doors through which you step into the myth-world of creative imagination. You make the story anew each time you confront the symbols.

DIVINATORY SIGNS

The *I Ching* also seeks to tell you which actions are helpful, and which are not, in any given situation. To do this, it often relies on a special kind of word called a *Divinatory Sign*. These words are like road signs which give directions and indicate the road conditions. They are used over and over again throughout the book to teach you how to follow the way.

The way is open and **the way is closed** are the most important signs. They indicate whether or not what you are asking about is in accord with the *tao*. Another important phrase is **there is a connection to the spirits**. It indicates that energy from deep sources and guiding spirits is available to help you and will carry you through. The signs **fault** and **without fault** talk about your motives. **Fault** indicates that you are not thinking honestly or clearly about the matter at hand, so someone may be hurt by what you do. **Without fault** shows your motives are true and that no harm will result from your action.

The sign **shame and confusion** points at the experience of temporarily losing the way. **Repenting** is a dissatisfaction with your conduct, a heart divided against itself. **Repenting disappears** and **without repenting** indicate either that the action in question can be done wholeheartedly, or that it leads to a healing of the divided heart.

Adversity shows danger with its roots in the past, a kind of danger represented as an angry ghost that seeks revenge on the living. It can be an old memory, a past situation, an evil deed, anything that returns to threaten or 'haunt' you. Usually we are told we must go through this danger and deal with it. Sometimes we are told to flee, for it is too powerful to be confronted. An **error** results from our ignorance or misperception; a **calamity** falls on us from outside like a plague or a flood. The direction **Step into the Great River** tells you to enter the stream of life with a purpose or goal, to begin a new enterprise or project. **Chastising** indicates both establishing order through discipline, rules and punishments and setting out on a purposeful expedition or trip.

Finally, there is a central set of divinatory signs that are found throughout the book in various combinations. These terms are very old, and were undoubtedly a magical formula that could open the gates to the spirit world. They can represent a seasonal cycle of time, the four directions, four key actions or four cardinal virtues. In divination, their earliest use, they are translated as: **Fundamental Success: Advantageous Divination.** All are thought of as very powerful words.

Fundamental refers to the primal originating power. It also means great, very much, excellent, potent, the head of a river and the source of thoughts. In the calendar it refers to spring, the east, sunrise. It often occurs with the term *the way is open* to become **the way is fundamentally open**, a very favourable outlook that contains the power to originate things.

Success refers to achievement, and offering a sacrifice to the spirits who are the source of that achievement. It indicates that something will be prosperous, vigorous and effective, full of life, fully grown and mature. It will spread, increase and reach a successful conclusion. In the calendar it is summer, the south, midday. **Success** often occurs coupled with a specific action, particularly the name of a Figure.

Advantageous refers to profit, benefit, insight and acute perception, harvest, a good outcome, all sorts of gain and gathering. In the calendar it is autumn, the west, sunset. This term usually occurs with other words that indicate specific actions in the phrase: **It is advantageous to** (do a certain thing). An action that is extremely beneficial for everyone and everything concerned is described by the phrase: **There is nothing for which this will not be advantageous.**

Divination refers to the result of a question put to the oracle. It also means to hold firm, keep on, put your ideas or plans to the trial. It indicates what is proven, righteous and firm. This term will often announce an answer or be combined with **advantageous**, as in **Advantageous Divination.** This phrase shows that profit and insight will accrue from the action in question.

It is very important to remember that the *I Ching*, unlike Western thought, does not separate the everyday and the 'transcendental'. You will consistently find a mixture of spiritual observations and directions for being happy in everyday life. This is one of the book's great lessons. Human happiness and following the way are by no means mutually exclusive.

UNDERSTANDING THE ANSWERS

The answer to the question you have posed the oracle will come primarily through the words of the 64 Figures. Let us take a sample question, and read through the texts.

A Sample Reading
I was consulted by a woman about whether or not she should leave her job and start a business of her own. She had a specific idea and the resources to begin. But there were important psychological and spiritual issues involved, about independence, fear, relations with other people and doubts about her ability. She wanted to do it, but did not know if she could or should. She asked 'What about starting a business on my own?' The answer was *40 Loosening* with one transforming line (9/4) giving the relating Figure *7 Legions*.

```
6 [ ___  ___ ]                          [ ___  ___ ]
5 [ ___  ___ ]                          [ ___  ___ ]
4 [ ____o____ ]         transforms to   [ ___  ___ ]

3 [ ___  ___ ]                          [ ___  ___ ]
2 [ _____ ]                         [ _____ ]
1 [ ___  ___ ]                          [ ___  ___ ]
```

Primary Hexagram	*transforms to:*	**Relating Hexagram**
Name: *40 Loosening*		Name: *7 Legions*

THE NAME AND ITS MEANINGS

When we look at Figure 40 we see that first of all it has a Name. This name describes the situation and indicates a basic way to act. Just beneath the Name, there are a few **keywords** that summarize the basic action. This is followed by the entire field of possible meanings that surround the Name.

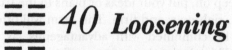 **40 Loosening**

Solve problems, untie knots, release blocked energy; liberation, end of suffering.

- **NAME**

Loosening/deliverance, HSIEH: divide, detach, untie, scatter, sever, dissolve, dispel; analyse, explain, understand; free from constraint, dispel sorrow, eliminate effects, solve problems; discharge, get rid of; take care of needs. The ideogram portrays a sharp horn instrument used to loosen knots.

This establishes the basic feeling of the answer. The situation is one of Loosening, so in order to connect with the time you must take things apart to release bound energy. This established an immediate rapport with the questioner. Starting the new business could solve problems, release her from tension or suffering, provide for her needs, explain and let her understand many of her conflicts.

THE IMAGE

This is the next part of the Figure. The literal translation would be 'head', for the Chinese word shows a pig's head, a sign of riches and good fortune. It gives basic directions for dealing with the situation described by the *Name* and shows how it may develop. After the *Image* there is a short explanatory paragraph. This is a combination of traditional commentary and modern observations and gives you the meaning of any obscure words or phrases.

- **IMAGE**

Loosening.
The south-west *is* advantageous.
If you have no place to go, the return is coming, the way is open.
If you have a direction to go, *begin* at daybreak, the way is open.

This is a release from tension and difficulty. It brings rousing new energy. Untie knots, solve problems, free energy. Joining with others (the southwest) will bring profit and insight. If no problems confront you, simply wait for the energy to return. The way is open. If you have something left to do, do it quickly. This will bring achievement. The way is open. This is a very fortunate situation. Forgive and forget, enjoy the new freedom. Stir things up and let go of constraints. By going on, you can gather crowds around you. Heaven and Earth loosen things through thunder and rain, and the seeds of all plants burst forth. This is truly a great and arousing time.

The sign *the way is open* occurs twice here, indicating that both staying still and finishing what is at hand as quickly as possible will open the way and the flow of energy. We are also told that joining with others for mutual benefit (the meaning of 'south-west') will bring advantage, profit and insight. All this is set in the atmosphere of loosening, freeing, liberating and separating things. This very much strengthened the sense that beginning the new business would bring release from tension and would liberate new energy. It advised her to involve others in her project and to begin it as soon as possible.

OUTER AND INNER WORLDS
This is a short analysis of how the two three-line Figures or trigrams interact with each other, and shows how energy is flowing between them. This relies on the actions traditionally asociated with the trigrams.

- **OUTER AND INNER WORLDS:** *Shake* and *Gorge*.
  Inside old structures are dissolving. This releases rousing new energy in the outer world.

Here we see that her old structures of thought, how she conceives of herself and her world, are already dissolving. This releases a burst of rousing energy that can manifest in the new activity.

HIDDEN POSSIBILITY
This gives you the Nuclear Figure hidden in the centre of this situation, along with a clue as to what the hidden meaning might be.

- **HIDDEN POSSIBILITY:** *63 Already Fording*.
  Loosening things and waiting for deliverance contains the hidden possibility that the action is already under way.

Here we see that everything is already in place for the liberating move. It may, in fact, be already under way.

SEQUENCE
This puts the Figure in sequence with the one that comes before it, seeing them as one action calling up another.

- **SEQUENCE**
  You are not allowed to complete hardship.
  Acknowledging this lets you use Loosening.
  Loosening implies relaxing.

Hardship refers to the previous Figure, *39 Difficulties*, and here we find that hardship cannot go on forever. If you realize this, you can use the energies of *Loosening*, which means to *relax* your hold on things. This gave us insight on the background to the question. Her previous position had become more and more difficult to deal with, and in order to cope she was holding on to herself very tightly. The new venture would allow her to let go and rediscover herself.

DEFINITION

This gives a concise one-word explanation of the Name, pointing out what can be a key quality.

> ● **DEFINITION**
> Loosening *means* relaxing.

This reinforced the basic reading. It was definitely time to relax her grip. The action she was thinking about could let her do this. It was the way to success in this situation.

SYMBOL

The symbol comes from another sort of tradition. It puts the symbols of the two trigrams together in order to deduce what the *realizing person*, the ideal user of the oracle, would do in such a situation.

> ● **SYMBOL**
> Thunder and rain arousing. Loosening.
> The realizing person forgives excess and pardons offences.

Thunder and rain, the symbols of the trigrams *Shake* and *Gorge*, have come together in order to arouse all things to new growth. The realizing person echoes this action in the human world by forgiving and pardoning oppressive people.

This answer seemed very favourable. The new venture could release her from tension, wipe out past difficulties, release new energy, relax her attitude towards life. She was advised to do what had to be done in order to begin it as soon as possible, and to forget the past, to forgive and forget. The way was open. The Hidden Possibility revealed that everything may already be in place for the new endeavour. We generated the Opposing Figure, which was 37 *Dwelling People*. It showed that her situation did *not* call for staying within the family or her usual circle of friends.

TRANSFORMING LINES

Up to this point we have just made general observations. The next part of the Figure, the Transforming Lines, shows us in detail where and how the Change takes place. This can, in fact, entirely contradict the basic meaning.

In the answer to this particular question there was just one transforming line, in the fourth place. This is a point of transition, where something inner, a plan, a feeling or desire, first manifests in the outer world. So it is particularly relevant when asking about the beginning of a new enterprise. This line reads:

• NINE AT FOURTH
Loosening *your* thumbs.
Partners come in the end,
Splitting apart brings a connection to the spirits.

Break from what you usually depend on. Friends and helpers will come in the end. The initial separation will connect you to the spirits.

We asked just who or what the 'thumbs' were. What did she depend on to grasp things, to understand or reach out? How was she all tied up? This was a time to set out alone, breaking away from things she unconsciously depended on. This 'splitting apart' is exactly the thing that would connect her to the spirits and her own inner power. It would assure her deliverance. Have no fear, the oracle said, the friends and partners you need will come in the end, *after* you have started on your own way. This kind of observation gives a very specific character to the general advice.

CHANGE PATTERN
We then generated the Change Pattern connected with this one line transforming; it was *9 Small Accumulating*. So the Change will proceed through amassing small things to achieve something great. She should not expect a dramatic breakthrough, but could feel assured that in the end the Change would be successful.

RELATING FIGURE
Finally, we looked at the Name and Image of the Relating Figure.

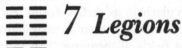 **7** *Legions*

Discipline, organize into functional units, mobilize, lead; master of arms.

• NAME
Legions/leading, SHIH: troops, an army; leader, general, master of arms, master of a craft; organize, make functional, mobilize, discipline; take as a model, imitate. The ideogram portrays people moving around a centre.

• IMAGE
Legions.
Divination: experienced people open the way.
Without fault.

This is a time to organize things into functional units so that you can take effective action. Put things in order. Develop the capacity to lead. Consult people with experience. Have a martial spirit. Remember, the ideal of this army is not to wage aggressive war, but to serve, to bring order and protect people who cannot protect themselves. It founds cities and defends what people need to live. This is not a mistake. You are surrounded by crowds of unorganized things. Take care

to correct this by giving each thing its place. Support and sustain the people.
This is difficult work. Take risks and confront obstacles in your desire to
serve. This activates a central principle people will spontaneously adhere to.
It is exactly what is needed. How could it be a mistake?

Here we find another kind of message. This is the kind of energy and
activity that can 'trigger' the basic Change. The new venture can
release rousing new energy and solve problems. There is a definite
chance of success on all levels, practical, personal and spiritual. But
to implement the new plan the inquirer will need new organization
and the aid of people who are experienced in the field. These may
be the new partners that will come to her. Through this organization
she will be able to use the energy released by the original idea.
When she needs help it will be there.

THE RESULT
Starting alone, and venturing quite outside her usual sphere of
activity, this woman gradually built up a flourishing business. The aid
she needed at critical times was always there, often in an unexpected
form. She is now in an entirely new circle of friends and partners and
is considerably happier with her work and her life.

TRANSLATING MAGIC

Spirit Words
This brings up the problem of translation. The Chinese written language was created by diviners. Particularly in its earliest forms, each
character or ideogram is a picture of something 'seen' in imaginative
vision that invokes several different fields of meaning. The words
were produced to communicate with the spirits, to call up their presence in the imagination, so they are much like the spirits themselves:
they can take many forms and have many meanings without losing
their essential identity.

Each word, when it stands alone, can be a noun, adjective, adverb,
or a verb in any of its tenses or persons. It is a *field* of action. This is
particularly true of the *names* of the 64 Figures. *Loosening*, for example, can mean: I, you, he, she, it, we or they loosen, loosened, are
being loosened, have loosened, have been loosened, will loosen or
will be loosened. It can also mean someone who loosens things, or to
do something in a 'loosening' way. In combination with other words,
it preserves much of this ambiguity. Take, for example, the phrase
'loosening dreams'. This can mean that we loosen dreams, let them
go, or that our dreams are loosened in us. It can also mean that the
dreams are of the 'loosening' kind, that is, they themselves do
the loosening.

Word Play

The point is that these words and phrases can be entered from many angles. They can be put on like a costume or a part in a play, through which we 'enter into the spirit' of the unfolding drama. You should keep this in mind as you read the words of the oracle. The sentences refer to an object or event that was 'symbolized' long ago. In many cases we can find the event or object to help in putting the words together. In some cases a long tradition guides us. We also know that the oracle was probably made as if it were talking to the individual who asks the question. All these things have played a part in the translation of the words and sentences in this book. It seeks to give you a real sense of the quality of the original language and the possibilities that branch off from each word, while making the impact of its sentences as clear as they would have been to one of the original users of the text.

In the texts, all the words in normal type come from the original. Each Chinese word is always translated by the same English word. The sentences tend to be concise and laconic, like proverbs, folk sayings, mantras, omens or spells. Each is a sort of 'eternal moment' that shows how transitions in time are made. The words in *italics* are implicit in the original. They have been added to help you understand the impact of the phrase. The translation is as close as possible to the meanings and feeling of the old oracle book.

The Stone in the Water

Keep this quality in mind when you read and use the texts. Think about them in their different forms and feel what they might connect with in your own experience. In a way, you translate these words again each time you use the oracle. A good image for the process is that of throwing a stone into water. The stone is your question. When you throw it, there is a strong, sudden moment of impact. This is the feeling of intuitive connection you will feel when you first see the text that answers your question. Then the circles of associations spread out in the water, penetrating into all the different parts of the subject. This is when, in the words of the traditional texts, you 'turn and roll the words in your heart', letting all the possibilities and persons arise. Finally you feel the intuitive connection confirmed by this process of thinking and feeling through things. The water becomes still. The message has penetrated and subtly re-arranged your imagining. You are ready to move with the way.

QUICK GUIDE:

Reading the Figures

Your question will be answered by one or more of the 64 Figures. They are built up of different kinds of sentence and diagram. Here is a quick key to understanding the various parts.

- Diagram, Name and keywords: The six-line diagram represents the Figure as a whole and lets you access it. The Name shows the overall theme or action of your answer, with the keywords beneath it picking out key facets. The definitions which follow give you the many different circles of meaning for the Name. Read all these to feel the basic atmosphere of your answer.

- The *Image* tells you what kinds of action and attitude are helpful in this situation and gives you the general direction of the movement. The paragraph beneath is a commentary from traditional and modern sources.

- *Outer and Inner Worlds* shows you what the interaction of the two three-line figures which make up the diagram means in this situation. This describes how your inner life connects with outer events.

- *Hidden Possibility* gives you the meaning of the Nuclear Figure. It shows a potential or warning hidden in the heart of the situation.

- *Sequence* puts the action of this Figure in sequence with the one that came before it. It shows what the situation was previous to your question and what you should understand and accept in order to use the energies of the present situation.

- *Definition* gives a concise one-word explanation of the *Name*.

- *Symbol* puts the symbols of the two three-line figures together to show what the *realizing person*, the ideal user of the oracle, would do in this situation.

- *Transforming Lines* (indicated as a 6 or a 9 at any one of the six places) show the precise points of Change, where and how things are happening. Look to them for an indication of how to move, the stages of a unfolding action, a warning of danger or assurance of success.

- The *Relating Figure*, generated if you have any transforming lines, shows how you are related to the basic answer. It can show a feeling, a tactic, a warning, a memory, a goal, a future development, a perspective or a deep concern. Read only the Name and Image of the Relating Figure.

- You can generate any one of the secondary figures to help you understand the basic situation. These include the *Opposing Figure*, the *Steps of Change*, and the *Change Pattern*.

PART TWO

The 64 Shapes of Change

THE SHAPES OF CHANGE BY NAME AND NUMBER

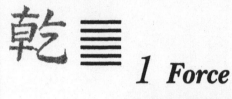

1 *Force*

Strength, creative energy, action; the power of heaven to create and destroy; dynamic, untiring, tenacious, enduring.

- **NAME**

Force/persisting, CH'IEN: spirit power, creative energy, forward motion; dynamic, enduring; firm, stable; activate, inspire; heaven, masculine, ruler; strong, robust, tenacious, untiring; *also*: exhaust, destroy, dry up, clear away. The ideogram portrays rising energy, the sun and growing plants.

- **IMAGE**

Force, Fundamental Success: Advantageous Divination.

This is the primal power of spirit to create and destroy. You see it in the light of heaven, the sun that makes everything grow, the fertilizing rain and the shape-changing energy of the dragon. You are confronted with many obstacles. Take action and persist in it. You are in contact with fundamental creative energy. Be dynamic, strong, untiring, tenacious and enduring. Ride the dragon and bring the fertilizing rain. This opens a new cycle of time. It will bring success, profit and insight. This great force begins things. You can use it to continue without pause. It shows you that the end is always a new beginning. The way of force is to transform things. It makes the innate spirit in each thing manifest. Ride the six stages of this energy. Use it to produce ideas that inspire people. What you create can be the source of a deep and self-renewing peace of mind.

- **OUTER AND INNER WORLDS:** *Force* and *Force.*

Dynamic, creative struggle, persistent and unwearied, characterizes the Force. There is great creative potential.

- **DEFINITION**

The Force *means* strength.

- **SYMBOL**

Heaven moves persistingly.
The realizing person uses *this* originating strength not to pause.

Transforming Lines

- **INITIAL NINE**

Immersed dragon, do not make use *of it.*

Your creative power is immersed in the waters below. You cannot use it yet. Have no fears, however. It is there and already working.

- **NINE AT SECOND**
See the dragon in the fields.
It is advantageous to see the Great Person.

Your creative energy appears in a field of activity. Your ability to realize things spreads. See people who can help you understand what is great in the world and in yourself. This will bring profit and insight. Let your central idea permeate things.

- **NINE AT THIRD**
The realizing person completes the day, force, force.
At nightfall, there are alarms like adversity.
Without fault.

A time of incessant activity. This is a transition. There are alarms all night long. It feels very dangerous. This is not a mistake. Turn your back on your former life. This is the return of the way.

- **NINE AT FOURTH**
Perhaps *someone* is playing in the abyss.
Without fault.

Play with things, even though they seem very serious. Do not let yourself be fixed in place. Your creative energy is certainly advancing.

- **NINE AT FIFTH**
A flying dragon in the heavens.
It is advantageous to see the Great Person.

Spread your wings. Your creative energy has been recognized. You have found a visible field of activity. See people whose influence can help you. Understand what is great in yourself. Let your idea unfold. Make things, build things, create and found.

- **NINE ABOVE**
An overbearing dragon, there will be repenting.

There is a difference between creative force and arrogance. Do not try to enforce your authority. You will most certainly have cause to regret it.

- **ALL NINES**
See the flock of dragons without a head. The way is open.

The inherent power of the spirit is blocking the emergence of a leader. Accept it. If you do not try to impose your ideas, the way is open.

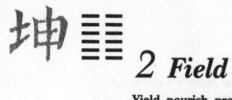

2 Field

Yield, nourish, provide; the power to give form to all things; receptive, gentle, giving, supple; welcome, consent.

- ## NAME
Field/yielding, K'UN: the surface of the world; concrete existence, the fundamental power to give things form; earth, moon, mother, wife, servants, ministers; supple strength, receptive power; welcome, consent to, respond to, yield, give birth, bear fruit; agree, follow, obey; nourish, provide, serve, work for. The ideogram portrays the spirits of the earth.

- ## IMAGE
Field. Fundamental Success: Advantageous Divination for the mare.
The realizing person has a direction to go.
At first there is delusion, then there is acquiring.
It is advantageous to *find* a lord.
In the Western South you acquire partners.
In the Eastern North you lose partners.
Divination: quiet *acceptance* opens the way.

This is the primal power to nourish and give things form. You see it in the earth, the moon, the mother, the devoted servant, the mare. You are confronted with many conflicting forces. Yield to each thing and give it form. Nourish and provide for it. This can open a whole new cycle of time. It brings success, profit and insight. Make sure you keep your sense of inner purpose. At first you will be confused by the profusion of events. Do not worry. Do whatever presents itself to be done. You will soon acquire what you need. It will bring profit and insight to work in a supporting role. Join with others in concrete activities (southwest). But do not shirk your own responsibilities (northeast). The way is open to you through calm, quiet acceptance. Let your power to realize things be so generous that it can carry everything that approaches. Cherish each thing and help it grow.

- ## OUTER AND INNER WORLDS: *Field* and *Field.*
Yielding, sustaining and serving govern the Field. There is a great potential to give things form.

- ## DEFINITION
The Field *means* suppleness.

- ## SYMBOL
Earth power. Field.
The realizing person uses munificent power and virtue to carry *all* the beings.

Transforming Lines

- **INITIAL SIX**
Treading the frost culminates in hardening the ice.

Act slowly, carefully and persistently to establish a solid base. Something important is returning.

- **SIX AT SECOND**
Straight, on all sides and Great.
Do not repeat *things*.
There is nothing for which this will not be advantageous.

Proceed directly and sincerely. Reform the crooked, extend to all sides, focus on a great idea. You have no need to rehearse or repeat things. Go right to the point. Everything will benefit from this. The power of the earth shines through it.

- **SIX AT THIRD**
Divination: a containing composition makes *things* possible.
If perhaps you are an adherent of a king's affairs there will be completion but no accomplishments.

Act through a design that contains and conceals. This is the place of hidden excellence. If you do not succumb to the need to have your accomplishments recognized, you can bring even serious affairs to completion. This is a far-reaching time. If you think of what is distant, you will be enlightened.

- **SIX AT FOURTH**
Bundled in the bag.
Without fault, without praise.

A time pregnant with possibility. There is nothing to praise or blame. What you desire is already there. Consider things carefully.

- **SIX AT FIFTH**
A yellow lower garment. The way is fundamentally open.

Humbly accept hidden processes. This may be confusing, but it will fundamentally open the way. Have patience. What is happening now will affect you deeply and positively.

- **SIX ABOVE**
Dragons struggle in the countryside.
Their blood is indigo *and* yellow.

Sky power and earth power are fighting, exhausting themselves in needless struggle. Yield, give way, restore peace. Strip away your ideas of power.

- **ALL SIXES**
Divination: perpetually advantageous.

A long-term effort from which great benefit will flow.

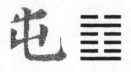

3 Sprouting

Beginning of growth and its problems; gather your strength; establish, found, assemble.

- **NAME**

Sprout, CHUN: begin or cause to grow; assemble, accumulate, amass, hoard; establish a base of operations, establish troops at the borders; difficult, painful, arduous; the difficulties at the beginning of an endeavour. The ideogram portrays a young plant breaking through the crust of the earth.

- **IMAGE**

Sprouting.
Fundamental Success: Advantageous Divination.
Do not make use of having a direction to go.
It is advantageous to install helpers.

This is a time of beginning growth, like young plants breaking through the covering earth. Assemble energy for the difficult task ahead. This can open a whole new time. It brings success, profit and insight. There are many new things emerging. Do not try to force things into a preconceived pattern. Install helpers and delegate responsibilities. That will bring profit and insight. Stake out your territory, assemble the troops, collect your possessions for the work ahead. Get rid of old ideas and let everything come into view. Set up structures that weave things together. There is heavy work to be done. Rouse your energy to confront the task. The atmosphere is the dusky light before daybreak and things are coming at you on all sides. Do not try to stop it. Install your helpers and give everything its place. This chaos is the beginning of a brand new world.

- **OUTER AND INNER WORLDS:** *Shake* and *Gorge.*

A cycle is ending in the outer world, while the new cycle sprouts within.

- **HIDDEN POSSIBILITY:** *23 Stripping.*

The new energy in sprouting contains the hidden possibility of stripping away outmoded forms.

- **SEQUENCE**

There is Heaven and Earth, then the myriad beings truly give birth.
Truly, the myriad beings.
Fill the space between Heaven and Earth to overflowing.
Acknowledging this lets you use Sprouting.
Sprouting implies filling *something* to overflowing.
Sprouting implies *that* the beginning of all being is giving birth.

- **DEFINITION**

Sprouting *means* being seen and not letting go of your residence.

- **SYMBOL**

Clouds and thunder. Sprouting.

A realizing person uses the canons to co-ordinate *things*.

Transforming Lines

- **INITIAL NINE**

A stone pillar.

Divination: residing in place is advantageous.

It is advantageous to install helpers.

The stone pillar is a grave post. Establish foundations rooted in the past. Empower people to help you. That brings profit and insight. Your purpose is moving correctly.

- **SIX AT SECOND**

When you sprout, then you quit.

You are riding a horse, fully arrayed.

The people you face are in no way outlaws, seek matrimonial alliances.

Divination: the woman will not nurse *a child*.

After ten years revolve, she will nurse *one*.

Every time you start something, you hit an obstacle and quit. What you are facing is not hostile. Make an alliance. It will take a long time to bear fruit, but stick with it.

- **SIX AT THIRD**

Approaching a stag lacking precaution.

Namely, you enter into the centre of the forest.

The realizing person almost fails to put this aside.

Going on brings shame and confusion.

You do not know what you are doing. You may lose your way even with this warning. If you go on, you will only see shame and confusion. Stop now. Listen to this advice.

- **SIX AT FOURTH**

You are riding a horse, fully arrayed.

Seek matrimonial alliances.

Going opens the way.

There is nothing for which this will not be advantageous.

You are fully arrayed, ready to go. Seek out alliances. Go forward, the way is open. Everything will benefit from this.

- **NINE AT FIFTH**

Sprouting: your juice.

Divination: the Small opens the way.

Divination: the Great closes the way.

You have the juice, the source of wealth. Give it to what needs it. That opens the way. Do not impose your will. That closes the way. Something great is returning.

- **SIX ABOVE**

You are riding a horse, fully arrayed,

And weeping blood is coursing down.

You are ready to go, yet standing still. Blood courses down and flows away. This is a terrible situation. Why let it go on any further?

4 *Enveloping*

Immature, young, unaware; concealed, hidden; nurture hidden growth, apprenticeship.

• NAME
Envelop, MENG: cover, hide, conceal; lid, covering; dull, unaware, ignorant, uneducated; young, undeveloped, fragile; unseen beginnings; *also*: a parasitic magical plant. The ideogram portrays a plant and a cover. It suggests nurturing hidden growth.

• IMAGE
Enveloping, Success.
In no way do I seek the youth *who is* enveloped.
The youth *who is* enveloped seeks me.
At the initial oracle consultation he is informed.
By asking two or three times, he obscures it.
If it is obscured, there is no information.

This is a time to stay concealed in order to nourish hidden growth. You are immature, and your understanding is dull and clouded. Accept being hidden to nurture the growing power of awareness. Put the lid on the situation. Pull the covers over. You do not know what you are doing yet. If you keep asking the same question, you will just muddy the waters. The beginnings are there even if you cannot see them. You already have an answer. Work on it. It will educate you. It will bring you success. What you see as an obstacle is really protecting your inner growth. That is why aggressive action is blocked. Use your confusion to envelop the premature desire to act. When you can really understand this, you will certainly become wise.

• OUTER AND INNER WORLDS: *Gorge* and *Bound*.
An outer limit hides and shields inner growth.

• HIDDEN POSSIBILITY: *24 Returning*.
Concealment and immaturity contain the hidden possibility of returning to the sources of energy.

• SEQUENCE
Something giving birth is necessarily enveloped.
Acknowledging this lets you use Enveloping.
Enveloping implies being enveloped.
It means that something is immature.

• DEFINITION
Enveloping *means being both* disordered and conspicuous.

• SYMBOL
Below the mountain spring water issues forth. Enveloping.
The realizing person uses fruitful movement to nurture power and virtue.

Transforming Lines

• INITIAL SIX
Far-reaching envelopment.
It is advantageous to punish people.
Loosen the fettering shackles *on the youth.*
Going on *like this* brings shame and confusion.

Correct the way you extend enveloping. Punishing real criminals certainly brings profit and insight, but you are holding your youthful energy on much too tight a rein. Loosen the shackles. Going on like this just brings shame and confusion.

• NINE AT SECOND
Enwrapped *and* enveloped. The way is open.
Let in the wife. The way is open.
The son *can* control the dwelling.

Enveloping becomes caring for and protecting. This opens the way. Take in a wife. This opens the way. The young son is mature enough to sustain and uphold the dwelling.

• SIX AT THIRD
Do not make use of *this* grasping woman.
She sees a metal (*golden*) husband
Who does not have a body.

Do not marry or connect with this person. Do not deal in idealized and inhuman images of wealth and power. You will lose your independence and the power to express yourself. There is nothing of value here. Beware.

• SIX AT FOURTH
Confining envelopment.

Enveloping turns to confining oppression and cuts you off from reality. Correct your thinking and return to the way.

• SIX AT FIFTH
Youthful envelopment. The way is open.

You are young and your awareness is enveloped. Because you accept this, all will go well. The way is open. It will lead to real understanding.

• NINE ABOVE
Smiting the envelopment.
It is not advantageous to act like an outlaw.
It is advantageous to resist outlaws.

This conflict is of your own making. You are attacking what envelops you and, consequently, it strikes back. Resist the temptation to rebel, break rules and act violently. This will bring you profit and insight. Use the time you organize yourself.

5 Attending

Wait for, wait on; attend to what is needed; watch for the right moment; participant in a sacrifice.

• NAME

Attend, HSÜ: take care of, look out for, serve; necessary, need, call for; provide what is needed; wait for, hesitate, doubt; stopped by rain; know how to wait, have patience and focus. The ideogram portrays rain and a sign that means both stop and source. It suggests being forced to wait and the ability to bring rain.

• IMAGE

Attending, there is a connection to the spirits.
Shining Success, Divination: the way is open.
It is advantageous to step into the Great River.

This is a time to wait for things and attend to what is needed. Find out what the situation requires. Wait for the right moment to act. There is a connection to the spirits here that will bring a brilliant success. You are like a participant in an important ceremony. The way is open. It is the right time to step into the stream of life with a purpose, to start a project or found an enterprise. Illuminate the situation through your repeated efforts. Attend wholeheartedly to the needs at hand. There is something immature here that must be nourished. Eating and drinking together with others is in harmony with the spirit of this time. It is not the time to advance yourself, champion a cause or climb a mountain. Help leisure, peace of mind, pleasure and harmony permeate the situation. Have patience. This is not an exhausting burden, it is how to act justly in the situation. It will connect you to the spirits above and bring you praise and accomplishment.

• OUTER AND INNER WORLDS: *Force* and *Gorge.*
Inner concentration confronts outer danger through attentive waiting.

• HIDDEN POSSIBILITY: *38 Diverging.*
Attending on something contains the hidden possibility of turning diverging opinions into creative tension.

• SEQUENCE
When *something* is immature you are not allowed not to nourish *it.*
Acknowledging this lets you use Attending.
Attending implies the way of eating and drinking.

• DEFINITION
Attending *means* not advancing.

- **SYMBOL**

Clouds above heaven. Attending.
A realizing person drinks and eats to repose and delight.

Transforming Lines

- **INITIAL NINE**

Attending in the outskirts.
It is advantageous to persevere.
Without fault.

You are at the outskirts heading toward the centre. This is heavy going. Endure in your efforts. It will bring profit and insight. This is not a mistake.

- **NINE AT SECOND**

Attending on the sands.
The Small has words.
Completing *this* opens the way.

Waiting on the sands, the shore laid bare by receding water. There is small talk and small people all around you. Adapt to it. The source is located in the centre and that is where you are headed. Going through with this opens the way.

- **NINE AT THIRD**

Attending in the bogs.
In the end *this* will involve outlaws.

You are bogged down and in danger. Being vulnerable like this will invite outlaws to take advantage of you. Think about it carefully. You still have time. Try to understand what you did to create this situation.

- **SIX AT FOURTH**

Attending in blood.
Issue forth from its origin in the cave!

You are in immediate danger. Get out of the cave now! You can save yourself if you will only listen.

- **NINE AT FIFTH**

Attending at *drinking* liquor and eating.
Divination: the way is open.

Join with others in eating and drinking. This is a ceremonial meal to which the spirits are invited. It will correct your isolation. The way is open. It separates the worthy from the unworthy.

- **SIX ABOVE**

Enter into the cave.
There will be visitors *who come* without being urged.
There are three people coming.
Respect them, completing *this* will open the way.

Go into your enclosed place. There are three unknown visitors coming. If you respect them, they will open the way and bring you answers to your problem.

6 Arguing

Dispute, controversy, argument; express your position; resolve or retreat from conflict.

• NAME
Argue, SUNG: dispute, plead your case, demand justice, contend in front of the ruler or judge; lodge a complaint, begin litigation; quarrels, wrangles, controversy; correct, reprimand, arrive at a judgement, resolve a conflict. The ideogram portrays words and the sign for official; pleading in front of authority.

• IMAGE
Arguing, there is a connection to the spirits. Restrain *your* alarm. Centring opens the way. Completing closes the way.
It is advantageous to see the Great Person.
It is not advantageous to step into the Great River.

This is a time to express your viewpoint clearly without taking aggressive action. If you cannot win the argument in that way, resolve or retreat from the conflict. There is a connection to the spirits in the situation, so do not become alarmed. Above all, keep your centre. Do not be carried away by anger or passion. This opens the way. Taking an argument through to the bitter end closes the way. See people whose influence can help you. Recognize what is great in yourself. This brings profit and insight. It is not the time to start a project or enter the stream of life with a purpose. There are too many contradicting movements. It is not a harmonious time. It is full of contradicting people and ideas. Do not try to bring everything together. Heaven is preparing something new. Express your own view and see what it brings. Be ready to retreat or compromise if necessary.

• OUTER AND INNER WORLDS: *Force* and *Gorge.*
Without a solid inner base, outer force can only be expressed through words.

• HIDDEN POSSIBILITY: *37 Dwelling People.*
Retreating from conflict contains the hidden possibility of finding the fellow feeling of people in a dwelling.

• SEQUENCE
When there is eating and drinking there is necessarily arguing. Acknowledging this lets you use Arguing.

• DEFINITION
Arguing *means* not connecting.

• SYMBOL
Heaven associates with the stream, contradicting movements. Arguing.
The realizing person arouses affairs to plan *new* beginnings.

Transforming Lines

• **INITIAL SIX**
This is not a perpetual place for affairs.
There are Small words, completing *them* opens the way.

This is not a place you want to stay in. Use whatever words you need to adapt and free yourself. Getting out of the situation will open the way.

• **NINE AT SECOND**
Do not *seek* control through arguing.
Convert *your position* and escape to *your* capital, to *your* people's three hundred doors.
Without error.

Do not try to control the situation. Change your goals and leave now. Go back to the place where people's doors are open to you, even if you must sneak away. This is not an ignorant mistake. When the distress comes to an end, you can reap the rewards of your timely return to yourself.

• **SIX AT THIRD**
Eating ancient power and virtue.
Divination: completing the adversity opens the way.
If you are perhaps an adherent of the affairs of a king, they will be without accomplishment.

Take in the power and virtue of the ancient sages. Confronting and conquering the danger with its roots in the past will open the way. You will not be able to accomplish a mission from your superior. Hold on to your own values.

• **NINE AT FOURTH**
Do not *seek* control through arguing.
Return, fate is approaching.
Divination: denial *and* quiet open the way.

Do not try to control the situation. Return to your own place and wait. A new fate is approaching you. Denying your current involvements and quieting your heart will open the way. Something important is returning to you. Do not let go of this chance.

• **NINE AT FIFTH**
Arguing, the way is fundamentally open.

Present your case with confidence and expect positive results. The way is fundamentally open. Correct your situation. It will bring results.

• **NINE ABOVE**
Perhaps a pouched belt is bestowed on you.
Complete dawn three times and you will be deprived of it.

If you think you can triumph in this situation, think again. Your prize will be taken away within three days. Acting like this is not worthy of you. It brings you no respect at all.

7 *Legions*

Discipline, organize into functional units, mobilize, lead; master of arms.

• NAME
Legions/leading, SHIH: troops, an army; leader, general, master of arms, master of a craft; organize, make functional, mobilize, discipline; take as a model, imitate. The ideogram portrays people moving around a centre.

• IMAGE
Legions.
Divination: experienced people open the way.
Without fault.

This is a time to organize things into functional units so that you can take effective action. Put things in order. Develop the capacity to lead. Consult people with experience. Have a martial spirit. Remember, the ideal of this army is not to wage aggressive war, but to serve, to bring order and protect people who cannot protect themselves. It founds cities and defends what people need in order to live. This is not a mistake. You are surrounded by crowds of unorganized things. Take care to correct this by giving each thing its place. Support and sustain the people. This is difficult, grievous work. Take risks and confront obstacles in your desire to serve. This activates a central principle people will spontaneously adhere to. It is exactly what is needed. How could it be a mistake?

• OUTER AND INNER WORLDS: *Field* and *Gorge*.
An inner willingness to risk and the outer goal of serving combine to make the legions.

• HIDDEN POSSIBILITY: *24 Returning*.
The organization of the legions contains the hidden possibility of returning to the source of energy.

• SEQUENCE
Whenever there is arguing crowds will rise up.
Acknowledging this lets you use the Legions.
Legions imply crowds.

• DEFINITION
Legions *mean* grieving.

• SYMBOL
In the earth centre there is a stream. Legions.
The realizing person tolerates the commoners to accumulate crowds.

Transforming Lines

• INITIAL SIX

The legions issue forth using regulations.
Obstructing virtue closes the way.

The legions need regulations to move, but make sure the regulations do not block their essential power and virtue. That would close the way.

• NINE AT SECOND

Located in the centre of the legions, the way is open.
Without fault.
The king bestows a mandate *on him* three times.

This is the leader's position, in the centre of the troops. It is not a mistake to be here. You will receive a mandate from the king three times. This is a great honour. Carrying out these orders will change your life.

• SIX AT THIRD

Perhaps the legions are carting corpses.
The way is closed.

Corpses are dead bodies, old memories, useless ideas or false images. In any case, get rid of them. What you are carrying around with you is closing the way.

• SIX AT FOURTH

The legions rest on the left (*the side of peace*).
Without fault.

The legions go the way of peace. This is not a mistake.

• SIX AT FIFTH

There are birds of prey in the fields.
It is advantageous to hold on to *your* words. Without fault.
If the elder son conducts the legions,
While the junior son carts corpses,
Divination: the way is closed.

The field is full of enemies. Hold on to your words and keep your own counsel. In this way, taking action will not be a mistake. Act as the eldest son who leads the legions into battle. Do not act as the junior son who carries corpses. Get rid of those old ideas and false images. If you cannot, the way will be closed to you. Acting for someone else or delegating responsibility is not appropriate here.

• SIX ABOVE

The Great Leader has a mandate.
He lays out the city and receives the dwellings.
Do not use Small People.

The great leader receives a mandate to found a city and allot the dwellings. He will be its patron. Do not be flexible now. You are in the correct position to achieve something great. It will necessarily upset the way power is currently apportioned. Do not worry. Do what you have to do.

8 Grouping

Alliance, mutual support, spiritual kin; how you group things and people; changing groups.

• NAME

Group, PI: join together, ally yourself with; people who are spiritually connected; find a new centre; order things in classes, compare and select; find what you belong with; harmonize, unite; neighbours; equal, identical; work together, work towards. The ideogram portrays a person who stops and looks around to examine things.

• IMAGE

Grouping, the way is open.
Retrace the oracle consultation *to make* the divination fundamental and perpetual.
Without fault.
This is not soothing, it comes on all sides.
For the man *who is* late the way is closed.

This is a time to look at whom you are grouped with and how you group things. Grouping can be a heartfelt connection, a spiritual bond. Look into the essential qualities of things. Compare and sort them according to their kind. To make your own connection to things and people clear, go over why you asked your question. Do not be afraid to ask again. This is not a soothing time. Things are changing radically and coming at you from all sides. Relationships are dissolving and re-forming. It is an important transition. If someone comes too late, the way will be closed. Get rid of your old ideas. You must find new ways to group things. This does not have to be painful. Let delight, harmony, elegance and pleasure be a key. Give each thing a place where it can joyously join with others. Connect your ideals to an underlying support. Take advantage and change now. If you put it off, the way will be closed.

• OUTER AND INNER WORLDS: *Gorge* and *Field*.

The relation to the outer world dissolves, while new ways to group things appear in the inner field.

• HIDDEN POSSIBILITY: *23 Stripping*.

Grouping things according to their qualities contains the hidden possibility of stripping away outmoded forms.

• SEQUENCE

Crowds must have a place to group.
Acknowledging this lets you use Grouping.
Grouping implies groups.

• DEFINITION

Grouping *means* delight.

SYMBOL
Above earth there is the stream. Grouping.
The early kings installed helpers to connect and rank the
myriad cities.

Transforming Lines

• INITIAL SIX
There is a connection to the spirits in this group.
Without fault.
There is a connection to the spirits that fills the jar to overflowing.
In the completion *that is* coming, there is even more of a
connection to the spirits.

*There is a connection to the spirits that brings this group together. This is not a
mistake. Pour in more. The waves of energy just keep coming.*

• SIX AT SECOND
Inside the origin of grouping.
Divination: the way is open.

*You are inside the group, and its origin has a place in you. The way is open. Do not
let this connection slip through your fingers.*

• SIX AT THIRD
A group of worthless people.

You are grouped with the wrong people. Leave before they do you real harm.

• SIX AT FOURTH
Outside the group.
Divination: the way is open.

*You are outside the group. The way is open to you. You are in this position because
of your moral and intellectual worth. Stick to your work and your values.*

• NINE AT FIFTH
A manifestation of grouping.
The king uses beaters on three *sides of the hunt.*
Letting go the game that goes before.
The capital's people are not admonished.
The way is open.

*To enact your desires, be like the king who goes hunting. Do not close all the avenues
of escape. Then, what is caught has chosen to be with you. This sets a shining
example. You do not have to scold people to make them obey you. The way is open.
You are in the right position to act.*

• SIX ABOVE
A group without a head.
The way is closed.

*A group with no leader is like a ship with no rudder. Both are going nowhere fast.
The way is closed. Leave this group or face disaster.*

9 *Small Accumulating*

Accumulate small things to do something great; adapt to each thing that crosses your path; nurture, tame, support, collect.

- **NAME**
Small, HSIAO: little, common, unimportant; adapt to what crosses your path; take in, make smaller; dwindle, lessen; little, slim, slight; yin energy.
Accumulate, CH'U: gather, collect, take in, hoard, retain; control, restrain; take care of, support, tolerate; tame, train or pasture animals, raise, bring up, domesticate; be tamed or controlled by something. The ideogram portrays the fertile black soil of a river delta.

- **IMAGE**
Small Accumulating, Success.
Shrouding clouds, *but* no rain.
It originates in my Western outskirts.

You are confronting a great variety of things that do not seem to be related. Take in each thing as it comes in order to accumulate something great. You must take the long view. Think of yourself as raising children, growing crops or taming animals. Be flexible and adaptable. Tolerate and nourish things. The clouds are gathering, rolling in from the West where rain begins. Successful completion is not far away. You can accumulate an enduring force. Focus on the inherent beauty of each thing in order to see its power. Persist in your efforts through gentle penetration. Praise and let go of what you have now, so the process can go on. The clouds are spreading. The time to act is not far off.

- **OUTER AND INNER WORLDS:** *Penetrating and Force.*
An enduring force accumulates within by gently penetrating each outer event.

- **HIDDEN POSSIBILITY:** *38 Diverging.*
Gathering small things to achieve a goal contains the hidden possibility of turning diverging opinions into creative tension.

- **SEQUENCE**
Grouping necessarily has a place to accumulate.
Acknowledging this lets you use Small Accumulating.

- **DEFINITION**
Small Accumulating *means at first there are* few.

- **SYMBOL**
The wind moves above heaven. Small Accumulating.
A realizing person highlights the pattern of power and virtue.

Transforming Lines

- **INITIAL NINE**
You return to the origin of the way.
How can this be a fault? The way is open.

Right at the beginning, you return to the way. How could this be a mistake? The way is open. Gently penetrate to the core of things.

- **NINE AT SECOND**
You return hauled along on a leash. The way is open.

You are dragged back like an animal on a leash. This opens the way. Do not let go of this source.

- **NINE AT THIRD**
The spokes of the cart are loosened.
The husband and *his* consort roll their eyes.

The cart cannot go forwards because the husband and wife are arguing, rolling their eyes at each other. Trying to carry a heavy load has brought on a family quarrel. This is not the way to put your house in order. Find your own centre before you move on.

- **SIX AT FOURTH**
There is a connection to the spirits.
Blood departs, alarm issues forth.
Without fault.

You can act with confidence. There is a connection to the spirits that will help you. In this way, any cause for bloodshed or alarm will disappear. This is not a mistake. Your purpose is united with those above.

- **NINE AT FIFTH**
There is a connection to the spirits, thus you are bound *to others.*
You can use your neighbour's affluence.

You are connected to the spirits and they will help you by binding you with others like the links in a chain. In this way, you will be able to use your friends' wealth as your own. Take hold of things. Be active.

- **NINE ABOVE**
There is already rain, *and* you already abide
in honour, power and virtue – carry on.
Divination: adversity for the wife.
Be like the moon *that* is almost full.
If the realizing person chastises, the way will close.

The rain has come. You abide in an honoured place and have power and virtue. Carry on as you are. This situation brings danger with its roots in the past that the wife must confront. Be like the moon almost full, never too much, always humble. If you try to assert yourself, discipline people or set out on an aggressive expedition, you will close the way. There is still something doubtful here.

10 Treading

Find and make your way, step by step; conduct, manners, salary, support.

• NAME
Tread, LÜ: walk, step; path, track, way; shoes; walk on, walk in the tracks of, follow a path; act, practise, accomplish; conduct, behaviour; salary, means of subsistence; happiness, luck; the paths of the stars and planets. The ideogram portrays a person's feet walking.

• IMAGE
Treading on a tiger's tail.
It does not snap at people. Success.

This is the time to find and make your way. Proceed carefully, step by step. The path is there. Think about the right way to act and gain your livelihood. There is a powerful force in front of you. You are walking in the tracks of the tiger. If you are careful and perceptive, this being will give you what you need to exist and frighten off what wants to harm you. Speak to it and you can partake of its power and intelligence. Do not do anything to make it bite you. You cannot afford to sneer and scold. This will bring you success. Meet the outer struggle cheerfully. This harmonizes and develops your ability to move with the way. Clarify your relation to the desires people hold in common. The impulse to movement you feel now can connect you with something important. Do not be disheartened. Continuing your efforts will bring a profound change.

• OUTER AND INNER WORLDS: *Force* and *Open.*
Inner stimulation and cheer alternate with outer struggle, marking the steps along the path.

• HIDDEN POSSIBILITY: *37 Dwelling People.*
Finding your way in the world contains the hidden possibility of a group of people to dwell and work with.

• SEQUENCE
Beings accumulate, then they have codes *to follow.*
Acknowledging this lets you use Treading.

• DEFINITION
Treading *means* not abiding.

• SYMBOL
Heaven is above, the mists below. Treading.
The realizing person differentiates the above and the below.
The realizing person sets right the commoners' purpose.

Transforming Lines

• **INITIAL NINE**
Treading *and* going simply.
Without fault.

Simply go your way. Be pure in your intent. This is not a mistake. You are moving with your desire.

• **NINE AT SECOND**
Treading the way, smoothing, smoothing.
Divination: *for* shadowed people the way is open.

You are treading the way, going over and over, smoothing things out. Do not be discouraged if this involves a lot of work. This brings profit and insight to people who are in retirement, hidden away from public life or working on their own.

• **SIX AT THIRD**
Someone who squints can observe.
Someone with a halting gait can tread.
They tread on a tiger's tail *and* he snaps at them.
The way is closed.
This is like a soldier acting as a Great Leader.

This is not the way to act. You do not have enough power or knowledge. You will step on the tiger's tail and be bitten. The way is closed. This is like a common soldier acting like a great leader. Do it only if you have received orders and it cannot be avoided.

• **NINE AT FOURTH**
Treading on a tiger's tail.
Pleading, pleading, completing *this* opens the way.

You tread on the tiger's tail. You meet the great person. You encounter the source of power. Be careful and courteous, but present your case with vigour and persuasive power. Going through with this will open the way. Your purpose is truly moving.

• **NINE AT FIFTH**
Decisive treading. Divination: adversity.

Be decisive and forge onward, even if you must part with something. You will confront danger with its roots in the past. Take action. Correcting the situation is definitely the right thing to do.

• **NINE ABOVE**
Observe your treading, the predecessors *are* auspicious.
Their recurring fundamentally opens the way.

Look at the path you have been walking. Your predecessors are extending their blessings. Where they recur and you have walked in their footsteps, the way fundamentally opens. Here you have reached the top. Your purpose will bring great rewards.

11 Pervading

Prospering, expanding, great abundance and harmony; peace, communication; spring, flowering.

• NAME
Pervade, T'AI: great, eminent, abundant, prosperous; peaceful, fertile; reach everywhere, permeate, diffuse, communicate; smooth, slippery; extreme, extravagant, prodigious. Mount T'ai was where the great sacrifices were made that connected heaven and earth. The ideogram portrays a person in water, connected to the flow of the *tao*.

• IMAGE
Pervading.
The Small *is* going, the Great *is* coming.
The way is open, Success.

This is an influx of spirit that brings ever-widening prosperity and flowering. You are connected to this flow. You can spread the prosperity by communicating. What is small and unimportant is leaving. What is great and important is coming. This gives you the chance to develop your fundamental ideas in an encouraging, stimulating atmosphere. Expand your involvement and pass the energy on. The way is open now. It will bring success and ripen everything. Be active. Reach out and penetrate to the heart of things. Radically renew your sense of yourself and who you associate with. Support and encourage people. This is the time when the fundamental powers mingle with humans and all can connect with one another. Be firm and focused within and adaptable in your dealings with other people. Have no doubt. This way will endure.

• OUTER AND INNER WORLDS: *Field* and *Force.*
An enduring force spreads from within, pervading and fertilizing the earth. This is a time of creative abundance.

• HIDDEN POSSIBILITY: *54 Converting the Maiden.*
Prosperity and expansion contain the hidden possibility of realizing your own potential.

• SEQUENCE
Treading and pervading, then quieting.
Acknowledging this lets you use Pervading.
Pervading implies interpenetrating.

• DEFINITION
Obstruction *and* Pervading reverse *who* you are classed *with.*

• SYMBOL
Heaven and Earth mingle. Pervading.
The crown prince uses property to accomplish Heaven and Earth's way.
The crown prince braces and mutualizes Heaven and Earth's propriety.
The crown prince uses the left (*peace*) to right the commoners.

Transforming Lines

- **INITIAL NINE**
Pull up the intertwisted thatch grass *by* using its classification.
Chastising opens the way.

Take vigorous action to advance from a lowly place, with and through others of your own kind. Order things and set out. The way is open. Let it take you into the world.

- **NINE AT SECOND**
Enwrapped by a wasteland.
Cross the channel. Do not put off leaving.
Your partners disappear.
You acquire honour by moving to the centre.

Surrounded by wasteland, at the edge of a river. Cross it. Do not put off leaving where you are. Your friends will disappear. You acquire honour by doing this.

- **NINE AT THIRD**
Without the even, *there is* no uneven.
Without going, *there is* no returning.
Divination: drudgery *is* without fault.
Have no cares, there is a connection to the spirit.
There is blessing in eating.

After level times, come difficult times. But without letting go, there will be no return. The drudgery you are facing is no mistake. Have no fear. You are connected to the spirits and they will help you. They will bless you and give you food in plenty.

- **SIX AT FOURTH**
Fluttering, fluttering.
If you are not affluent, use your neighbour.
This is not a warning, use your connection to the spirits.

Fluttering like a bird trying to leave the nest. If you do not have what you need, use your friends. This is not to warn you. Use the connection to the spirits you already have. Do not worry about immediate gain. Centre your heart's desire and take flight.

- **SIX AT FIFTH**
The Supreme Burgeoning converts the maiden.
This brings satisfaction, the way is fundamentally open.

The Great Ancestor takes a maiden in marriage. A great omen of future happiness. This can gratify desires and realize your aims. The way is fundamentally open.

- **SIX ABOVE**
The bulwark returns to the moat. Do not avail of the legions.
An informing mandate originates from the capital.
Divination: shame and confusion.

The walls fall down. The prosperous city will fall. But do not call out the legions. This has fate and higher authority behind it. Fighting it will only bring shame and confusion. Your destiny is in disarray. You will need to concentrate anew.

12 *Obstruction*

Obstacle, blocked communication; decline, cut off, closed; late autumn.

• NAME
Obstruct, PI: closed, stopped, bar the way; obstacle; unable to advance or succeed; deny, refuse, disapprove; bad, evil, unfortunate, wicked, unhappy. The ideogram portrays a mouth and the sign for not. It suggests blocked communication.

• IMAGE
Obstruction *through* worthless people.
Divination: not advantageous for the realizing person.
The Great is going, the Small is coming.

This is a time when communication is blocked. You are being obstructed by people of little worth and petty aims. There is nothing advantageous in the situation. If you try to act, you will encounter resistance and misfortune. What you say will be rejected. You will be personally disapproved of or insulted. What is great and important is leaving; what is small and unimportant, concerned only with its own gain, is coming. This means you will not be able to realize your plans. You must adapt to the time and withdraw. You cannot always be part of a group. Change your idea of yourself and your associates. Do not mingle. Avoid responsibility. If you stay hidden, you can continue to draw benefits. This is a time of isolation and disconnection where you do not have a sphere of activity. It is not your fault. The people who run things think only of their own advantage. For now, their way will endure.

• OUTER AND INNER WORLDS: *Force* and *Field*.
An outer struggle blocks and confines inner productivity.

• HIDDEN POSSIBILITY: *53 Gradual Advancing.*
Accepting obstruction contains the hidden possibility of gradually achieving your goal.

• SEQUENCE
You are not allowed to completely interpenetrate *with others*. Acknowledging this lets you use Obstruction.

• DEFINITION
Obstruction and Pervading reverse *who* you are classed *with*.

• SYMBOL
Heaven and Earth do not mingle. Obstruction.
A realizing person uses power and virtue parsimoniously to cast out heaviness.
A realizing person does not allow splendour and *thus* can use his benefits.

Transforming Lines

- **INITIAL SIX**

Pull up the intertwisted thatch grass by using its classification.
Divination: the way is open. Success.

This is a time to go into retreat along with others of your own kind. The way is open to you. This will bring success and ripen your plans to return.

- **SIX AT SECOND**

Enwrap *what* you receive.
For Small People the way is open.
The Great Person is obstructed. Success.

Enwrap what you receive. Put it in the womb to bear fruit later. The way is open for people who adapt to whatever crosses their path. The person who has a central idea and the desire to see it through is obstructed now. The development allowed by this time of obstruction will bring success and ripen your plans.

- **SIX AT THIRD**

Enwrapped in embarrassment.

You will be wrapped in embarrassment if you go on like this. The time is not right for what you are doing. Examine yourself.

- **NINE AT FOURTH**

There is a mandate, without fault.
Cultivate this *in* radiant satisfaction.

This is given to you by fate to undertake. There is no mistake. Work at it. It is a great task in a difficult time. In the end, it will bring you joy and satisfaction. You will spread light to all.

- **NINE AT FIFTH**

Resting from the obstruction.
For the Great Person the way is open.
It disappears, it disappears:
Attach it to a grove of mulberry trees.

Let go. Do not fight the obstruction. If you have a real goal or central idea, the way will open to you. The obstruction is disappearing. Imagine yourself in a peaceful retreat. That is the right place for you. It will correct the whole situation.

- **NINE ABOVE**

Subverting the obstruction.
At first obstruction, afterwards rejoicing.

The obstruction is turned upside down. What was once an obstruction is now a cause to rejoice. Let the old time pass away. Why go on regretting things?

13 Concording People

Harmony, bring people together, share your idea or goal, welcome others, co-operate.

● NAME
Concord, T'UNG: harmonize, bring together, unite; union, concord, harmony; equalize, assemble, share, agree; together, held in common; the same time and place. The ideogram portrays a mouth and the sign for cover. It suggests silent understanding and things that fit together.
People, JEN: human beings; an individual; humanity. The ideogram portrays a person kneeling in prayer or submission.

● IMAGE
Concording People in the countryside. Success.
It is advantageous to step into the Great River.
Divination: advantageous for the realizing person.

This is a time to bring people together in view of a shared purpose or goal. Find ways to unite people. You are facing the kind of task that can best be done together and will bring mutual advantage, like planting, harvesting or building. Find out how goals and feelings may be shared. Now is the time to embark on a new project or found an enterprise. Step into the stream of life with a purpose. Focusing on the way and how to move with it will bring profit and insight. Warmth and understanding will help you in your struggle. People should not stay apart from each other. Think about how to connect them. Bring them together, for a creative force is moving in the centre of the group. Keep trying to see the inherent beauty of things and to move with the way. You can connect with the deep purposes that influence and move the world.

● OUTER AND INNER WORLDS: *Radiance* and *Force.*
Brightness and warmth radiate outward through people's effort to come together.

● HIDDEN POSSIBILITY: *44 Coupling.*
Bringing people together contains the hidden possibility of a spontaneous union of the two primal powers.

● SEQUENCE
You are not allowed to be completely obstructed.
Acknowledging this lets you use Concording People.

● DEFINITION
Concording People *means* connecting.

● SYMBOL
Heaven associates with fire. Concording People.
A realizing person sorts the clans to mark off the beings.

Transforming Lines

- **INITIAL NINE**
Concording people at the gate.
Without fault.

You are about to cross over the threshold. Take action. This is not a mistake. Walk through the door.

- **SIX AT SECOND**
Concording people in the ancestral hall.
Shame and confusion.

Gathered in front of the ancestral images and the ideals they represent, you feel the shame and confusion of having lost the way. This is precisely the right thing to feel. Let it induce reflection and correct the way you are thinking.

- **NINE AT THIRD**
Hiding arms in the thickets.
Ascending your high mound.
For three years' time you will not rise up.

You hide weapons in dense brush and climb your ancestral grave mound. You will not be able to act for three years. You are facing a very strong antagonist. Try to free yourself from these thickets of resentment.

- **NINE AT FOURTH**
Riding on your ramparts.
Nothing can impede *or* attack you.
The way is open.

You have built an invulnerable position. As you walk the walls of your city, nothing can hold you back or attack you. The way is open. Rouse things. Stimulate power and desire. This will reverse what might look like a confining situation.

- **NINE AT FIFTH**
Concording people first cry out and sob and then they laugh.
The Great Leader controls their mutual meeting.

People who wish to unite cry at first, then laugh together. Coming together is not always easy. Have a great organizing idea. Speak directly and clearly. Using words can unite these people into a group and empower them.

- **NINE ABOVE**
Concording people in the outskirts.
Without repenting.

People meet on the outskirts. There will be no cause for regrets. This group does not have a purpose yet. Peel off the dead skin and help find it.

14 Great Possessions

A powerful idea; great power to realize things; organize your efforts, concentrate; great results and achievements.

• NAME
Great, TA: big, noble, important; able to protect others; orient your will towards a self-imposed goal; the ability to lead or guide your life; yang energy.
Possess, YU: there is; to be, to exist; have, own; possessions, goods; dispose of; arise, occur, events. The ideogram portrays a hand holding an offering. It suggests sharing with the spirits and other people.

• IMAGE
Great Possessions, fundamental Success.

This is a time when you can acquire great abundance and prosperity through the development of a central plan or idea. Concentrate your energy. Focus on a single idea and impose a direction on things. Be noble and magnanimous with the results. This can be a deep and continuing source of success, excellence and fertility. Make a great offering and share it with others. By concentrating your inner force you can spread brightness and warmth. Be decisive. You gather the crowds around you. Firmly check hatred and negative emotion. Yield to the powerful spirit of the time and let go of your personal restrictions. Brighten the inherent beauty of things. This will connect you to heaven above and let you know the right moment to act.

• OUTER AND INNER WORLDS: *Radiance* and *Force.*
Great force concentrates within, spreading brightness and warmth in the outer world. This is a time of great abundance.

• HIDDEN POSSIBILITY: *43 Deciding.*
Focusing on a central idea and receiving the benefits contains the hidden possibility of clear and decisive action.

• SEQUENCE
Associating with concording people implies that beings are necessarily *and* truly converted *to your idea.*
Acknowledging this lets you use Great Possessions.

• DEFINITION
Great Possessions *means* crowds.

• SYMBOL
Fire is located above heaven.
A realizing person terminates hatred and displays improvement.
A realizing person yields to heaven and rests in his fate.

Transforming Lines

• INITIAL NINE
Without mingling harm.
This is in no way faulty.
The drudgery *involved* is by consequence *also* without fault.

There is nothing harmful in this idea. It is completely without fault. So the very hard work associated with it is also not a mistake. This is the beginning of a great endeavour.

• NINE AT SECOND
Use a Great chariot to carry *it*.
There is a direction to go. Without fault.

You need a great vehicle to carry out your plan. Dedicate yourself to the effort. There is a clear way to proceed. This is not a mistake.

• NINE AT THIRD
A prince makes a sacrifice to the Son of Heaven.
Small People *can* nowhere impede it.

Concentrate what you are doing and offer it to the highest principle you know. Do not try to adapt to circumstances. This will create a firm connection. Do not let others control your ideas.

• NINE AT FOURTH
In no way *seek* dominance.
Without fault.

Do not try to be forceful or dominant. The time is not right for that. Let others shine. Be very clear about this. It is not a mistake.

• SIX AT FIFTH
You *really* have a connection to the spirits!
If you mingle, then it will impress *others*.

Act with complete confidence. Your connection to the spirits will impress people the moment you contact them. Stay true to your purpose. This impressive ability has real meaning. Be versatile. Stay imaginatively open, rather than trying to prepare everything.

• NINE ABOVE
Heaven shields its origins.
The way is open.
There is nothing for which this will not be advantageous.

Heaven shields this from its birth. The way is open. Everything will benefit from it. It is blessed and protected by the spirit.

15 Humbling

Cut through pride and complications, keep close to fundamental things; be simple; think and speak of yourself humbly.

• NAME
Humble, CH'IEN: think and speak of yourself in a modest way; voluntarily give way to others, polite, modest, simple, respectful; yielding, compliant, reverent. The ideogram portrays spoken words and the sign for unite. It suggests keeping words connected to the facts.

• IMAGE
Humbling, Success.
For the realizing person there is completion.

This is a time to be humble and stay close to fundamental things. Cut through pride and complication. Keep your words simple. Think of yourself in a modest way. Voluntarily take the lower position. This will bring success. In this way you free yourself and can use an opponent's own strength against him. Use the oracle to keep in touch with the way and you will be able to bring your ideas to completion. Be clear about these things. Your inner limits connect you with the power of the earth. This releases you from constraint. Be agile and alert. Balance things carefully and correct any excess. This is a time of connection. Heaven moves below to bring brightness and clarity. Earth's modesty moves above. It is the way of all things to lessen what is overfull and to help and cherish the humble. It brings dignity and makes things shine. Through humbling you can accomplish and complete things.

• OUTER AND INNER WORLDS: *Field* and *Bound.*
Inner limits sustain yielding and serving on the wide field of the earth. Yin and yang come into creative balance.

• HIDDEN POSSIBILITY: *40 Loosening.*
A humble attitude contains the hidden possibility of being freed from tension and compulsion.

• SEQUENCE
Great possessions do not allow filling *things* to overflowing. Acknowledging this lets you use Humbling.

• DEFINITION
Humbling *means* agility.

• SYMBOL
In the earth centre there is a mountain. Humbling.
The realizing person reduces the numerous to augment the few.
The realizing person evaluates, evens and spreads out the beings.

Transforming Lines

• INITIAL SIX
The realizing person, humbling, humbling.
Step into the Great River. The way is open.

To stay in touch with the tao, be very humble. Think everything through twice. Use this attitude to step into the stream of life. Start a project. Found an enterprise. Through humbling, the way is open to you.

• SIX AT SECOND
Humbling calling out. Divination: the way is open.

Your inner power calls out to others. The way is open. Make a statement from the centre of your heart and you will obtain what you wish.

• NINE AT THIRD
The realizing person toils humbly.
There will be completion, the way is open.

Staying in touch with the tao, you toil humbly. Carry on. You do not need to advertise yourself. Bringing your work to completion opens the way. It mobilizes an undeveloped potential that will attract many people.

• SIX AT FOURTH
Demonstrating humbling.
There is nothing for which this will not be advantageous.

This action demonstrates what humbling really is. Everything will benefit from it. Show your ideas and achievements humbly and without attachment. Do not get involved in arguments.

• SIX AT FIFTH
If you are not affluent, use your neighbours.
It is advantageous to encroach *on them* and subjugate *them.*
There is nothing for which this will not be advantageous.

If you do not have what you need to carry out your plan, use your neighbours. Attack and subjugate them and take what you need. This is not a time for false modesty. Everything will benefit from this.

• SIX ABOVE
Humbling calling out.
It is advantageous to move the legions,
And chastise the capital city.

Your inner power calls out to others. No false modesty here. Mobilize your forces and attack the capital city. Now is the time to chastise the corrupt and put things in the right order. You can achieve your goal.

16 Providing For

Gather what you need to meet the future; able to respond immediately; enjoy, pleasure, enthusiasm, be carried away.

• NAME
Provide for/respond, YÛ: ready, prepared for; take precautions, arrange, make ready; happy, content, rejoice, take pleasure in; carried away, enthusiastic, respond immediately, ready to explode. The ideogram portrays a child riding an elephant. It suggests that being prepared lets you respond spontaneously.

• IMAGE
Providing For.
It is advantageous to install helpers to move the legions.

This is the time to build up strength and resources to meet whatever the future may bring. That way you can respond spontaneously and fully when the summons to action comes. You can take pleasure in things. Think things through so you can smoothly ride the flow of events. Install and empower helpers, so your forces can respond immediately to any situation. That will bring profit and insight. Your accumulated energy will bound out of the earth at a sudden call. Have a firm purpose and be adaptable to build up the capacity to respond. Amass a great store. This is how Heaven and Earth work together to create time and order the seasons. The old sages acted like this. They could respond immediately from their store of virtue and thus the people accepted them. The time to provide for a spontaneous response is righteous and great.

• OUTER AND INNER WORLDS: *Field* and *Shake.*
Inner labour accumulates the strength to respond quickly to a rousing call to action.

• HIDDEN POSSIBILITY: *39 Difficulties.*
Building up reserves to meet the unknown contains the hidden possibility of re-imagining a difficult situation.

• SEQUENCE
Great possessions and the ability to be humble necessarily provide for *responding to any situation.*
Acknowledging this lets you use Providing For.

• DEFINITION
Providing For *means there will be* indolence.

• SYMBOL
Thunder impetuously issues forth from the earth. Providing For.
The early kings aroused delight to extol power and virtue.
Their exalting worship of the Supreme Above was used to equal the grandfathers and predecessors.

Transforming Lines

• INITIAL SIX
Calling out for provision.
The way is closed.

Do not call out to others to provide for you. That closes the way. You will simply exhaust your own purpose. Wait and respond to a real call.

• SIX AT SECOND
The limits are turning to stone.
Do not *even* complete the day.
Divination: the way is open.

The limits you have set are so rigid they, and you, are turning to stone. Do not even complete one more day like this. The way is open to you. Correct yourself and release the bound energy.

• SIX AT THIRD
Sceptical providing for *brings* repenting.
Procrastinating has repenting.

Do not be sceptical and do not procrastinate. They will bring you sorrows and doubts. Provide for what is needed, directly and simply. You will not be sorry.

• NINE AT FOURTH
Previously provided for.
Great acquisitions.
Do not doubt.
You join partners together *as* a clasp *gathers the hair.*

Have no doubts. Everything is already provided for. You will acquire great things. You gather people together as a hair clasp gathers the hair, all eager to join for mutual joy and profit. Your purpose can move great things.

• SIX AT FIFTH
Divination: affliction.
Persevere, you will not die.

You are confronting sickness, hatred or disorder. Keep on. It will not kill you. You are riding a strong, persisting force that cannot be exhausted.

• SIX ABOVE
Dark providing for.
Deny your accomplishments.
Without fault.

You are moving in the darkness. Do not pretend you have accomplished anything. This situation is not your fault, but why let it go on any longer? Climb out of the cave.

17 Following

Be drawn into motion; influenced by, accept guidance; move with the flow, natural and correct.

- **NAME**

Follow, SUI: come or go after in an inevitable sequence; conform to, according to, come immediately after; in the style of, according to the ideas of; move in the same direction; follow a way, school or religion. The ideogram portrays three footsteps, one following the other.

- **IMAGE**

Following.
Fundamental Success: Advantageous Divination.
Without fault.

You are being drawn forward through a strong attraction. Follow the inevitable course of events. Yield to the path set out in front of you, the path of least resistance. Be guided by the way things are moving. You are involved in a series of events that are firmly connected. This can open up a new time. It will bring fundamental success, profit and insight. It is not a mistake. The call has come. Let go of what is past. A new focus is emerging. Dim your discriminating power so old habits can dissolve. The whole world must follow the times and the seasons. You are following a righteous idea inherent in the time.

- **OUTER AND INNER WORLDS:** *Open* and *Shake.*

Stimulating words in the outer world stir up new energy within. These trigrams emphasize taking new action.

- **HIDDEN POSSIBILITY:** *53 Gradual Advancing.*

Following a model, person or process contains the hidden possibility of gradually realizing your desires.

- **SEQUENCE**

Providing For necessarily *creates* a following.
Acknowledging this lets you use Following.

- **DEFINITION**

Following *is* without previous causes.

- **SYMBOL**

In the centre of the mists there is thunder. Following.
A realizing person turns to darkening to enter a reposing pause.

Transforming Lines

* **INITIAL NINE**

If you have an office, deny it. Divination: the way is open.
Issue forth from the gate and mingle *with others*.
There will be achievements.

Leave what you usually do, go out into the world and mingle with others. The way is open. By stepping out of your usual place you will achieve something.

* **SIX AT SECOND**

Tied to the Small son,
You let the respectable manager go.

You have chosen to follow the small child and let go of the responsible manager. You are alone, without associates, and must adapt to what crosses your path.

* **SIX AT THIRD**

Tied to the respectable manager,
You let the Small son go.
Following, you seek and acquire *what you desire*.
Divination: residing in place *is* advantageous.

You let go of the small child and follow the responsible manager. In this way, you will find what you desire. Staying where you are will bring profit and insight.

* **NINE AT FOURTH**

Following *in order* to capture *something*.
Divination: the way is closed.
If you connect to the spirits and locate *yourself* in *tao*,
Your *understanding* will be brightened.
How could that be faulty?

Following is not hunting. If you follow only in order to capture a specific thing, the way will be closed. Locate yourself in the way and open your heart to the flow of the spirits. Then you will understand what to follow. How could that be a mistake? Your righteous sense of purpose is leading you astray. This could be a new beginning.

* **NINE AT FIFTH**

There is a connection to the spirits leading to excellence.
The way is open.

The way is open to you. Follow the connection. It leads on to excellence.

* **SIX ABOVE**

Grappled and tied to it,
Thus the adherents are held fast to it.
The king makes a sacrifice on the Western Mountain.

You are firmly attached to what you follow, and others are held fast through you. You are enshrined in the hall of ancestors. You become a presence in people's imagination. This is as far as you can go.

18 Corruption

Disorder, perversion or decay with roots in the past, black magic; renew, renovate, find a new beginning.

• NAME
Corrupt/Renovating, KU: rotting, poisonous; intestinal worms, venomous insects; evil magic; seduce, pervert, flatter, put under a spell; disorder, error; business. The ideogram portrays poisonous insects in a jar used for magic.

• IMAGE
Corruption, fundamental Success.
It is advantageous to step into the Great River.
Before seedburst, three days; after seedburst, three days.

This is a time of corruption, decay and hidden poison. It contains the challenge to find the source of the corruption and deal with it, so a new time can begin. You are faced with something that has turned bad, like the evil deeds of parents that are manifested in their children. Search out the source and change it. This will bring fundamental success. Step into the stream of life with a firm purpose. This brings profit and insight. Prepare the change carefully. Watch over its beginnings, then guide its first growth. Doing business always implies corruption, but you can find its source. Rouse the undeveloped potential. This can produce a new spring and regulate the world once more. You will soon have more than enough to keep you busy. The spirit is moving in this situation.

• OUTER AND INNER WORLDS: *Bound* and *Penetrating*.
An outer limit turns growth in on itself, corrupting it.

• HIDDEN POSSIBILITY: *54 Converting the Maiden*.
Dealing with the source of corruption contains the hidden possibility of realizing your own potential.

• SEQUENCE
Using rejoicing to follow people necessarily implies there are affairs.
Acknowledging this lets you use Corruption.
Corruption implies affairs.

• DEFINITION
Dealing with corruption *brings* stability indeed.

• SYMBOL
Below the mountain there is wind. Corruption.
The realizing person rouses the commoners to nurture power and virtue.

Transforming Lines

- **INITIAL SIX**

Managing the father's corruption.
If there is a son the predecessors are without fault.
Adversity, completion opens the way.

You are dealing with the corruption of authority. If you act as a son, accepting your duty to change things, those who went before you will remain without blame. You are confronting danger with its roots in the past, like an angry old ghost. Going through the confrontation will open the way.

- **NINE AT SECOND**

Managing the mother's corruption.
This does not allow a divination.

You are dealing with the corruption of nourishment and care. Divination or good ideas will not help. You must put yourself in the middle of the situation and find the way. Then you will see the obstruction.

- **NINE AT THIRD**

Managing the father's corruption.
For the Small there will be repenting.
Being without the Great *is* a fault.

You are dealing with the corruption of authority. Those who co-operated with it will have sorrow and regrets. You must have a strong central purpose or you will make a grave mistake.

- **SIX AT FOURTH**

Enriching the father's corruption.
Going on *like this brings* shame and confusion.

You are adding to the corruption of authority. Going on like this only produces shame and the confusion of having lost the way.

- **SIX AT FIFTH**

Managing the father's corruption.
Use praise *to accomplish it.*

You are dealing with the corruption of authority. Do not attack directly. Use praise to accomplish what you want to do. In the process you will find your own purpose.

- **NINE ABOVE**

Do not *involve yourself in* the affairs of kings and helpers.
Honouring the highest is your affair.

Politics and business are not your concern. Your job is to find and honour what is most excellent in this world. This is the place of those who work on in the darkness to prepare the coming awakening.

19 Nearing

Approach, the arrival of the new, growing; an honoured and powerful force comes nearer.

• NAME
Nearing, LIN: approach, behold with care and sympathy; commanded to come nearer; look down on sympathetically, confer favour and blessing; inspect; arrive, the point of arrival, make contact; honour or be honoured by a visit.

• IMAGE
Nearing, Fundamental Success: Advantageous Divination.
An end in the eighth moon (*month*) closes the way.

Something significant is approaching. This is the point of first contact, the arrival of the new. This particularly describes the approach of something great and powerful to something smaller. Welcome the approach without immediately expecting to get what you want. Look after things with care and sympathy. Keep your expectations modest. This contact can open a whole new time. It brings fundamental success, profit and insight. This is a particularly favourable time for what is growing, so do not rush to complete things. This will not be an early harvest. It is the return of the great. Continually correct your path and ponder the deep concerns of the heart. That is heaven's way. Work to express it.

• OUTER AND INNER WORLDS: *Field* and *Open*.
Inner cheer and stimulation, combined with a willingness to serve in the outer world, invites nearing.

• HIDDEN POSSIBILITY: *24 Returning*.
The connection with what is nearing contains the hidden possibility of a return of fundamental spirit.

• SEQUENCE
There are affairs and then *this* allows the Great *to approach*. Acknowledging this lets you use Nearing.
Nearing implies the Great indeed.

• DEFINITION
Nearing and Viewing *are* righteous.
Perhaps you associate with *others*, perhaps you seek *them*.

• SYMBOL
Above the mists there is the earth. Nearing.
A realizing person teaches and ponders without exhaustion.
A realizing person tolerates and protects the commoners without limit.

Transforming Lines

- **INITIAL NINE**

A conjunction *is* nearing. Divination: the way is open.

An important connection is coming nearer. It will stimulate and inspire you. The way is open. Your purpose is moving.

- **NINE AT SECOND**

A conjunction *is* nearing, the way is open.
There is nothing for which this is not advantageous.

An important connection is coming nearer. It will stimulate and inspire you. There is nothing that will not benefit from this. You have not yet seen all the good consequences.

- **SIX AT THIRD**

Sweetly nearing.
There is no advantageous direction.
If you are already grieving over this you are without fault.

This approach looks sweet, but there is no way that good can come of it. It is just not right for you. If you have already realized this, you will make no mistake.

- **SIX AT FOURTH**

The culmination *is* nearing.
Without fault.

The climax is coming nearer. This is not a mistake. The time is right. Go for it.

- **SIX AT FIFTH**

Knowledge *is* nearing.
This is proper to a Great Leader.
The way is open.

Knowledge comes nearer, the knowledge that a great leader uses to help and influence people. This can change the basic way you see yourself and what is important to you.

- **SIX ABOVE**

Generosity *is* nearing.
The way is open. Without fault.

Wealth, honesty and generosity are nearing. Use these qualities and you will meet them in others. Hold on to your own inner purpose. You will get what you desire.

20 *Viewing*

Look at things from a distance, contemplate, let everything come into view, divine the meaning.

• NAME

View, KUAN: contemplate, look at from a distance or height; examine, judge, conjecture about; divination; idea, point of view; instruct, inform, point out, make known; *also:* a Taoist monastery, an observatory, a tower. The ideogram portrays a bird and the sign for see. It suggests a bird's eye view and watching bird signs.

• IMAGE

Viewing, the ablution and not the libation.
The connection to the spirit will come like a presence.

This is a time to look at things without acting in order to divine their meaning and find the right perspective. Let everything emerge. Look particularly at those things you usually do not want to see. This is the time in a religious ceremony when the purification has been made, and the libation or offering is about to be poured out. Have confidence. Looking into things will bring you the insight you need. The spirit will arrive and carry you through. Let all the images appear on the inner field of vision. Strip away your preconceived ideas. Seek out what is important. Yield to things and give them space on the inner ground. You can let your whole world come into view. If you prepare well, the things you are trying to influence will change spontaneously. When the sages used this way of teaching, the whole world would listen.

• OUTER AND INNER WORLDS: *Penetrating* and *Field.*

Entering the inner field, images of distant things and actions come into view.

• HIDDEN POSSIBILITY: *23 Stripping.*

Letting everything come into view contains the hidden possibility of stripping away what is outmoded.

• SEQUENCE

Being Great, you are allowed to view *things.*
Acknowledging this lets you use Viewing.

• DEFINITION

Nearing and Viewing *are* righteous.
Perhaps you associate with *others*, perhaps you seek *them.*

• SYMBOL

The wind moves above the earth. Viewing.
The early kings inspected on all sides, viewing the commoners to set up *their* teaching.

Transforming Lines

- **INITIAL SIX**

Youthful viewing.

For Small People *this is* without fault.

For a realizing person it *brings* shame and confusion.

You are looking at things like a child. This is fine if all you want to do is adapt to what crosses your path. If you want to follow the way, you should be ashamed of it.

- **SIX AT SECOND**

Furtive viewing.

Divination: advantageous for the woman.

Looking at things from hiding, secretly viewing and influencing things. This brings profit and insight if you choose to act like a woman, even if you see a few shameful things.

- **SIX AT THIRD**

Viewing my birth, advancing *and* withdrawing.

Look at your life and what you give birth to. Watch the flow as it advances and retreats. Then use that to answer your question, to see if you should go forward or go back.

- **SIX AT FOURTH**

Viewing the shining of the city.

It is advantageous to be the guest of the king.

You have been invited into an important advisory position. Take advantage of invitations from those above you. It will bring profit and insight. Proceed step by step. This is a long term experience.

- **NINE AT FIFTH**

Viewing my birth.

The realizing person *is* without fault.

Look at your life and what you give birth to. This can answer your question. Where you can really say you are without fault, you will see your higher self.

- **NINE ABOVE**

Viewing one's birth.

A realizing person *is* without fault.

View the lives and origins of those around you and see yourself as one of them. This can answer your question. Where you see someone acting without fault, you can see your higher self. Then decide whether or not to act. Your purpose is not clear yet.

21 Gnawing and Biting Through

Confront the problem, bite through the obstacle, be tenacious, reveal the essential.

• NAME

Gnaw, SHIH: bite away, chew, eat; nibble, bite persistently; arrive at, attain; reach the truth by removing what is unessential. The ideogram portrays a mouth and the sign for divination. It suggests finding the truth by divining what is hidden.

Bite through, HO: unite, bring together; close the jaws, bite through, crush, chew; the sound of voices. The ideogram portrays a mouth and a covered vessel. It suggests the jaws coming together as a lid fits a pot.

• IMAGE

Gnawing and Biting Through, Success.
It is advantageous to make use of litigation.

You are confronting a tough obstacle. It is as if something were keeping your jaws from coming together. Be determined. Gnaw away at the problem until you can bite through it. That way you reveal what is really there. Take decisive action. This will bring you success. Use the law and punishment where necessary. Insisting on your rights and going to judgement will bring profit and insight. Your determination can break through the obstacles and shed light on the situation. You have contemplated long enough. Now act. Gnaw and bite through!

• OUTER AND INNER WORLDS: *Radiance* and *Shake.*
A rousing inner force bites through the obstacle to spread awareness in the outer world. These trigrams emphasize taking action.

• HIDDEN POSSIBILITY: *39 Difficulties.*
Resolutely biting through obstacles contains the hidden possibility of re-imagining a difficult situation.

• SEQUENCE
When viewing is allowed, then there is a place to unite. Acknowledging this lets you use Gnawing and Biting Through. Gnawing and Biting Through implies uniting.

• DEFINITION
Gnawing and Biting Through *means* eating.

• SYMBOL
Thunder and lightning. Gnawing and Biting Through.
The early kings brightened the use of flogging to enforce the laws.

Transforming Lines

● **INITIAL NINE**
Locked in a wooden stock, *your* feet disappear.
Without fault.

You are locked up. You cannot move for now. This is a mild punishment. It is not a mistake to yield to it.

● **SIX AT SECOND**
Gnawing through flesh, *your* nose disappears.
Without fault.

You are very enthusiastically gnawing through the obstacle. This is not a mistake. Keep on.

● **SIX AT THIRD**
Gnawing through dried meat. You meet *something* poisonous.
The Small has shame and confusion.
Without fault.

Gnawing through old, tough stuff, you encounter something poisonous. Bring it out. Do not let go. If you try to simply adapt, you will know the shame of having lost the way. This steadfastness is not a mistake.

● **NINE AT FOURTH**
Gnawing through parched meat with bones.
You acquire a metal arrow.
Divination: drudgery is advantageous.
The way is open.

Examine the results of past efforts. Find what is there of worth. You will acquire the ability to direct your strength and give things form. The drudgery associated with this task will bring profit and insight. The way is open. Get to work.

● **SIX AT FIFTH**
Gnawing through parched meat.
You acquire yellow metal (*gold*).
Divination: adversity.
Without fault.

This is a long, arduous task, but the rewards will be great. You acquire wealth and the possibility to establish a line of descent. You will have to confront your own ghosts and shadows in the process, but doing this is not a mistake.

● **NINE ABOVE**
Why are you locked in a wooden stock so your ears disappear?
The way is closed.

This is a serious punishment. Why won't you hear and understand? The way is closed. Think again. You certainly won't be enlightened if you go on like this.

22 Adorning

Make outward appearance reflect inner worth; embellish, beautify, display courage and beauty to build inner value.

• NAME
Adorn, PI: embellish, ornament, beautify; elegant, brilliant; inner worth seen in outer appearance; energetic, brave, eager, passionate, intrepid; display of courage. The ideogram portrays cowrie shells, a sign of value, and flowers. It links worth and beauty.

• IMAGE
Adorning, Success.
For the Small *it is* advantageous to have a direction to go.

This is a time to decorate, embellish and beautify the way things look, including yourself. This builds up the intrinsic value and lets inner changes be seen. Be elegant. Be brilliant. Display your valour. It will bring you success. If you can adapt to things and not impose your will, having a plan will bring profit and insight. Make a radiant display. Brighten and clarify all the parts of the way you present yourself. Do not cut off things that are already underway. Reveal the strength of the underlying design. Use gradual change to accomplish what you want.

• OUTER AND INNER WORLDS: *Bound* and *Radiance.*
An outer limit restrains inner brightness and awareness to display.

• HIDDEN POSSIBILITY: *40 Loosening.*
Adorning your outward appearance contains the hidden possibility of being released from tension and compulsion.

• SEQUENCE
You are not allowed to unite and climax without *first* considering *it.*
Acknowledging this lets you use Adorning.
Adorning implies embellishing.

• DEFINITION
Adorning *starts* without a complexion.

• SYMBOL
Below the mountain there is fire. Adorning.
The realizing person brightens the multitude's standards without daring to sever litigation.

Transforming Lines

> • **INITIAL NINE**
> Adorning your feet.
> Put away the chariot and *go* on foot.

Go on by yourself. Adorn yourself with courage. Do not take the easy way out.

> • **SIX AT SECOND**
> Adorning your growing beard.

Be brave and patient. It will take time, but the connection to a superior is already there. It will lift you into a new sphere.

> • **NINE AT THIRD**
> Adorning as if you soak *yourself* in it.
> Divination: the way is perpetually open.

Soak yourself in this idea. Let it impregnate you. Do not try to bring it to an end. This can open the way for you and all your descendants.

> • **SIX AT FOURTH**
> Adorning as *if it were* old and venerable, like a soaring
> white horse.
> They are in no way outlaws, *seek* matrimonial alliances.

Adorn this idea with the respect due to venerable age and wisdom. It will give you the ability to fly high and manifest creative energy. The people approaching are not outlaws. Seek alliance with them. Do not use force.

> • **SIX AT FIFTH**
> Adorning in the hill-top garden.
> The roll of plain silk is little, little.
> Shame and confusion. Completing opens the way.

When you reach the shrine, you realize you have very little to give. You feel ashamed, and tempted to withdraw. Do not do it. Go through this to the end and it will open the way. It will give you a cause to rejoice.

> • **NINE ABOVE**
> White adorning.
> Without fault.

Adorn it in white, the colour of death, mourning and what is clear, plain and pure. This reveals the essentials. Acquire a noble purpose. This is not a mistake.

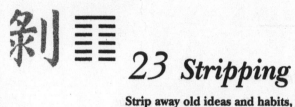

23 Stripping

Strip away old ideas and habits, eliminate what is unusable, outmoded or worn out.

• NAME
Strip, PO: flay, peel, skin, scrape, slice; remove, uncover, take off; reduce, diminish; reduce to the essentials; prune trees, slaughter animals. The ideogram portrays a knife and the sign for carving. It suggests taking decisive action to cut something away.

• IMAGE
Stripping, *it is* not advantageous to have a direction to go.

This is a time to strip away what is unusable, habits and ideas that have grown old and outmoded. Remove and uncover things. Cut into the problem and strip away the unessential. It will not bring you profit or insight to have a plan or a direction. Deal with what is at hand. This is the end of an old cycle and the preparation for the new. Re-establish creative balance by stripping away outmoded embellishments. Take action. Give generously to what is below you to stabilize your own position. Adapt to what is coming. Do not impose your will. Concentrate on the symbolic value of things, their power to connect with the spirit world. The old structure is dissolving so new action can emerge. That is where heaven is moving.

• OUTER AND INNER WORLDS: *Bound* and *Field*.
The outer limit strips away the previous cycle, while the new is being prepared on the inner field.

• HIDDEN POSSIBILITY: *2 Field*.
Stripping things away contains the hidden possibility of revealing a new field of action.

• SEQUENCE
Because *this* actually involved embellishing, growth is by consequence used up.
Acknowledging this lets you use Stripping.
Stripping implies *someone who* strips *things* indeed.

• DEFINITION
Stripping *means something is* rotten.

• SYMBOL
The mountain adjoins earth.
By being munificent, those above quiet the position of *those* below.

Transforming Lines

- **INITIAL SIX**

Strip the bed *by* using the stand.
Ignoring the Divination closes the way.

Change your resting place by changing your stand, your views about what supports you. If you ignore the call, the way will close.

- **SIX AT SECOND**

Strip the bed *by* marking *things* off.
Ignoring the Divination closes the way.

Change your resting place by clearly dividing yourself from others. Bite into it. You do not have the right associates yet. If you ignore the call, the way will close.

- **SIX AT THIRD**

Strip it! Without fault.

Strip it away, whatever it is. This is not a mistake.

- **SIX AT FOURTH**

By stripping the bed, you cut into the flesh.
The way is closed.

You are cutting too close. If you try to change your resting place this way, you will do someone real injury. You are slicing close to a calamity. This will close the way.

- **SIX AT FIFTH**

Threading fish *by the gills.*
Obtaining the favour of the women of the palace.
There is nothing for which this is not advantageous.

The fish who symbolize profit and fertility are hidden in the changing stream of events. String them together. The women of the palace will confer their grace and elegance. Honour them. Use your connections and trust your imagination. There is nothing that will not benefit from this.

- **NINE ABOVE**

A ripe fruit is not eaten.
The realizing person acquires a cart.
Small People *only* strip *their* huts.

The fruit is ripe, eat it. Take in the fruits of your actions. If you want to stay in touch with the way, develop the capacity to carry it away. Move on. Do not be adaptable and simply strip your hut in order to stay where you are.

24 Returning

Energy and spirit return after a difficult time; renewal, re-birth, re-establish; new hope.

• NAME
Return, FU: go back, turn back, return to the starting point; come back, reappear; resurgence, re-birth, renaissance; re-establish, renew, renovate, restore; again, anew; an earlier time and place; the very beginning of the new time. The ideogram portrays the signs for walking and retracing a path.

• IMAGE
Returning, Success.
Issuing forth and entering in without affliction.
Partners come without fault.
Your *tao* reverses and returns. Returning comes on the seventh day.
It is advantageous to have a direction to go.

This is a time of re-birth and returning energy after a difficult time. Go back to meet this new energy in order to begin anew. This will bring success. Return to the source. Restore the original purity and feeling. Things go out and come in without trouble or disturbance. People will suggest profitable projects. It is not a mistake to join them. Your way reverses direction and returns to you on the seventh day, at the end of the completed period of time. You can begin again. Have a plan or a direction. That will bring profit and insight. Be open to new ideas. Turn in your tracks to meet what is coming. Returning to the way is the root of virtue and power. Mark yourself off from others and nurture the returning energy. Stir things up and work with the movement. Let things emerge without pressure. Heaven is moving here. In returning, you see the heart of Heaven and Earth.

• OUTER AND INNER WORLDS: *Field* and *Shake.*
Rousing new energy germinates inside and opens a new field of activity.

• HIDDEN POSSIBILITY: *2 Field.*
The reappearance of creative energy contains the hidden possibility of giving everything new form and shape.

• SEQUENCE
You are not allowed to completely use things up.
When stripping is exhausted above, it reverses *itself* below.
Acknowledging this lets you use Returning.

• DEFINITION
Returning *means* reversing.

• SYMBOL
Thunder located in the earth centre. Returning.
The early kings barred the passages at sun's ending (*winter solstice*).

Sojourning merchants did not move at sun's ending.
The crown prince did not inspect on all sides at sun's ending.

Transforming Lines

● **INITIAL NINE**
Do not keep returning at a distance.
Do not merely repent.
The way is fundamentally open.

Do not merely talk about returning, do it. Go back to the source. The way is
fundamentally open if you do. It will renovate your whole being.

● **SIX AT SECOND**
Rest *through* returning.
The way is open.

Return to the source by relaxing your grip. Let things rest. Let go of what you are
doing. Be unselfish and benevolent. Recognize your common humanity. The way is
open to you.

● **SIX AT THIRD**
An urgent return. Adversity.
Without fault.

You return with a sense of urgency. You will confront dangers with their roots in the
past. Go on. This is not a mistake.

● **SIX AT FOURTH**
The centre is moving, return alone.

The centre of things is moving. You sense this and move with it, even though you
must go alone. Do not be sorry. You are following the way.

● **SIX AT FIFTH**
Generosity returns, without repenting.

Generosity, wealth and honesty return to strengthen you. Act through these qualities.
You will not have cause to regret it. The old wise men are behind
you, smiling.

● **SIX ABOVE**
Delusion returns.
There will be calamities and blunders.
If you try to move the legions, at the completion there will be
great destruction.
For the city and its leader the way is closed.
This will end in ten revolved years of uncontrolled chastisement.

Delusion, infatuation and self-deception return to blind you. This is a disaster.
If you move like this, all will be destroyed. Your city and its leader will be cut off
from the way. It will take ten years to deal with the repercussions of this catastrophe.
Think about where this desire comes from. Whatever it is, do not do it!

25 *Without Embroiling*

Disentangle yourself; spontaneous, unplanned, direct; clean, pure, free from confusion or ulterior motives.

- **NAME**
Without, WU: devoid of, not having.
Embroiling, WANG: caught up in, entangled, enmeshed, involved; vain, rash, reckless, foolish, wild; lie, deceive; idle, futile, without foundation, false; brutal, insane, disordered.

- **IMAGE**
Without Embroiling.
Fundamental Success: Advantageous Divination.
If you do not correct yourself, this will be an error.
Then it is not advantageous to have a direction to go.

This is a time to stay unentangled. Do not get caught up in things. If you are free from disorder, compulsion and vanity, you can act spontaneously and confidently. Free yourself from anger, lust and hatred or greed for gain. You gain the capacity to act directly. This can begin a new time. It offers fundamental success, profit and insight. If you do not correct yourself, however, you will continually make mistakes through ignorance or faulty perception. Then nothing you do will be of any use. Action now is inspired by the spirit of heaven. Proceed in this spirit, step by step. If you do that, success will be your fate. If you become entangled and lose the connection, how could you do anything right?

- **OUTER AND INNER WORLDS:** *Force* and *Shake*.
Inner growth remains free of entanglement through its continual connection to heaven.

- **HIDDEN POSSIBILITY:** *53 Gradual Advancing*.
Remaining free of entangling emotions contains the hidden possibility of gradually advancing to your goal.

- **SEQUENCE**
You actually return, by consequence you are not embroiled.
Acknowledging this lets you use Without Embroiling.

- **DEFINITION**
Without Embroiling *means* calamity *can only come from outside*.

- **SYMBOL**
Below heaven thunder moves. Beings associate Without Embroiling.
The early kings used the luxuriance that suited the time to nurture the myriad beings.

Transforming Lines

- **INITIAL NINE**

Without embroiling. Go *forward*, the way is open.

You are not caught up in negativity. The way is open. Go through with your plan.

- **SIX AT SECOND**

Not tilling the crop. Not clearing the ploughland.
By consequence it is advantageous to have a direction to go.

This is not the time or place to till a crop or clear new land. If you realize this, what you do will bring profit and insight. Move on. Wealth comes through other means.

- **SIX AT THIRD**

Without embroiling there is a calamity.
Perhaps there are tethered cattle.
If the moving people acquire them *it is* the capital
people's calamity.

An unfortunate occurrence. The cattle belonging to the city people have vanished. This is a calamity for them, but the nomads who took them acquire new strength and capacity. You can take your pick. Which would you rather be?

- **NINE AT FOURTH**

Divination: this is allowed.
Without fault.

An enabling divination. Go through with your plan. It is not a mistake.

- **NINE AT FIFTH**

Without embroiling, there is affliction.
If you do not use medicine, there will be rejoicing.

You are experiencing sickness, disorder or violent emotion. This is not your fault. Do not try to treat it literally or medically. Then you will see the reason for it and have cause to rejoice.

- **NINE ABOVE**

Without embroiling. There is error in moving.
No direction is advantageous.

Stay unentangled. It is an error to move at all. There is nothing you can do that will be to your advantage.

26 *Great Accumulating*

Concentrate, focus on a great idea; accumulate energy, bring everything together; a time for great effort and achievement.

• NAME
Great, TA: big, noble, important; able to protect others; orient your will towards a self-imposed goal; the ability to lead or guide your life; yang energy.
Accumulate, CH'U: gather, collect, take in, hoard, retain; control, restrain; take care of, support, tolerate; tame, train or pasture animals, raise, bring up, domesticate; be tamed or controlled by something. The ideogram portrays fertile black soil accumulated by retaining silt.

• IMAGE
Great Accumulating.
Advantageous Divination.
Do not eat in your dwelling (*or with your clan*). The way is open.
It is advantageous to step into the Great River.

Now is the time to accumulate things through the power of a great central idea. Focus on one thing and impose a direction on your life. Concentrate everything on this idea. It will bring you profit and insight. Gather all the many parts of yourself and your experience. Think of yourself as raising animals or growing crops. Tolerate and nourish what you accumulate. Do not stay at home or in your immediate circle of friends. The way is open to great things. Step into the stream of life with a purpose. Study the precedents and go on from there. Be firm, persist. Renew your connection to the way each day. Nourish moral and intellectual power. This is a great time. The connections reach to heaven.

• OUTER AND INNER WORLDS: *Bound* and *Force*.
An outer limit retains and accumulates heaven's great force. This is a time of strength and abundance.

• HIDDEN POSSIBILITY: *54 Converting the Maiden*.
The power that comes from great accumulating contains the hidden possibility of realizing your potential.

• SEQUENCE
Being without embroiling then allows you to accumulate *things*. Acknowledging this lets you use Great Accumulating.

• DEFINITION
Great Accumulating *means it is* the right time.

- **SYMBOL**

Heaven located in the mountain centre. Great Accumulating.
The realizing person uses numerous past records and
predecessors' words to move.
The realizing person accumulates power and virtue.

Transforming Lines

- **INITIAL NINE**

There is adversity.
It is advantageous to *bring this to* an end.

This is too dangerous. Stop now. It will bring you profit and insight.

- **NINE AT SECOND**

Loosening the cart's axles.

*This is a disconnection between the body and the wheels of the cart. Because of this,
you cannot go anywhere. Relationships have broken down and you cannot carry on.
You need a show of beauty and bravery to release the bound energy.*

- **NINE AT THIRD**

Pursuing a fine horse.
Divination: drudgery is advantageous.
It is spoken thus: you are escorting an enclosed cart.
It is advantageous to have a direction to go.

*You are pursuing something fine and spirited, an ideal. The drudgery you must go
through is worth it. Think of it this way: You are escorting a closed cart with your
secret hidden inside. Having a plan will bring you profit and insight.*

- **SIX AT FOURTH**

A stable for young cattle.
The way is fundamentally open.

*You accumulate the strength to carry heavy loads and the force to confront difficult
situations. This takes time, but the way is fundamentally open. This will give you
cause to rejoice.*

- **SIX AT FIFTH**

A gelded boar's tusks.
The way is open.

*A fierce enemy has been deprived of the capacity to harm you. The way is open, the
obstacle is gone. This will bring rewards.*

- **NINE ABOVE**

Is this heaven's highway? Success.

*In doing this, you walk heaven's highway. The way is moving in your idea. Have
no doubt about its success.*

27 Jaws

Nourishing and being nourished, food and words; the mouth, your daily bread; take things in, swallow.

• NAME

Jaws/swallowing, YI: mouth, jaws, cheeks, chin; source of nourishment; eat, take in, ingest; feed, nourish, sustain, bring up, support; provide what is necessary; what goes in or out of the mouth. The ideogram portrays an open mouth.

• IMAGE

The Jaws, Divination: the way is open.
View the Jaws,
Seek the origin of what really fills *your* mouth.

This is a time to look at what goes in and out of your mouth. Where do the words and the food come from? Where do they go? What is the source of your nourishment and whom do you nourish? Concern yourself with taking things in, literally and metaphorically. Take in what has been said and done to feed the new in yourself and others. Help to nourish people and their hopes and needs. Through these concerns, the way opens. Contemplate these things deeply, for the answer to your question lies there. Correct the source of nourishment. Articulate how you eat, drink and speak. Heaven and Earth nourish the myriad beings. The sages nourish what is excellent in order to extend it to others. You can do this also. This is a time to be great.

• OUTER AND INNER WORLDS: *Bound* and *Shake*.

Previous accomplishments are taken in to nourish germinating new energy.

• HIDDEN POSSIBILITY: *2 Field*.

Providing nourishment and taking things in contain the hidden possibility of giving form and help to all things.

• SEQUENCE

Beings accumulate, then you are allowed to nourish *them*.
Acknowledging this lets you use Jaws.
Jaws implies nourishing.

• DEFINITION

The Jaws *means* correcting nourishment.

• SYMBOL

Below the mountain there is thunder. Jaws.
The realizing person considers his words *when* he informs.
The realizing person articulates drinking and eating.

Transforming Lines

- **INITIAL NINE**

You simply put away your magic tortoise *and say:*
View my jaws hanging down. The way is closed.

What unnecessary melancholy! You put your imagination and your soul aside and say: Look how sad I am! This is what closes the way. It has no value whatsoever.

- **SIX AT SECOND**

Toppling the jaws.
Rejecting the canons, move to the hilltop.
The jaws, chastising closes the way.

Your connection to what nourishes you is disturbed. You have rejected the norms and standards. Move to your own hilltop shrine. Trying to discipline people in order to nourish yourself will only close the way.

- **SIX AT THIRD**

Rejecting the jaws. Divination: the way is closed.
You will not *be able* to act for ten revolved years.
There is no advantageous direction.

You are rejecting the source of your nourishment. The way is closed. If you go on, you will be out of action for ten years. There is nothing you can do that would bring you advantage. Your idea goes against the tao.

- **SIX AT FOURTH**

Toppling the jaws.
A tiger observes, glaring, glaring.
His passions, pursuing, pursuing.
Without fault.

Your connection to the source of nourishment is disturbed and toppling over. Find a new one. Be like the tiger, full of force and concentration, pursuing his passions. This is not a mistake. It will bring light and clarity to the situation.

- **SIX AT FIFTH**

Rejecting the canons.
Divination: residing in place opens the way.
This does not allow stepping into the Great River.

You are rejecting the norms that regulate people. The way will be open only if you stay where you are for now. This is not a time to start a new project or an enterprise. The impulse you are feeling, however, will connect you to what is above.

- **NINE ABOVE**

Previous jaws (*nourishment*). Adversity, the way is open.
It is advantageous to step into the Great River.

You are nourished by what came before you. Look at what happened in the past. There is danger that has its roots there. Now is the time to confront it. The way is open. Step into the stream of life with a purpose. Your ideas will be rewarded.

28 Great Exceeding

A crisis; gather all your force, don't be afraid to act alone; hold on to your ideals.

- ## NAME
Great, TA: big, noble, important; able to protect others; orient your will towards a self-imposed goal; the ability to lead or guide your life; yang energy.
Exceed, KU: go beyond; pass by, pass over, surpass; overtake, overshoot; get clear of, get over; cross the threshold, surmount difficulties; transgress the norms, outside the limits; too much.

- ## IMAGE
Great Exceeding, the ridgepole *of the house* is sagging.
It is advantageous to have a direction to go.
Success.

This is a time of crisis and transition. The structure of things is sagging to the breaking point. Do not be afraid to act alone. Push your principles and ideals beyond their normal limits. Have a noble purpose. Find what is truly important to you and organize yourself around it. Having a plan will bring profit and insight. Though the structure of things is in danger of collapse, there is a creative purpose at work in the breakdown. If your situation does not nourish you, if it will not support new growth, push it over and leave. The roots and the tips of things are fading. Let the strong force gathering in the centre penetrate and move you. This can be a very important time.

- ## OUTER AND INNER WORLDS: *Open* and *Penetrating*.
Deep inner penetration and outer stimulation lead to excessive concern with a great idea.

- ## HIDDEN POSSIBILITY: *1 Force.*
The time of crisis contains the hidden possibility of great creative energy.

- ## SEQUENCE
If *things* are not nourished, by consequence you are not allowed to stir *them* up.
Acknowledging this lets you use Great Exceeding.

- ## DEFINITION
Great Exceeding *means* toppling over.

- ## SYMBOL
The mists submerge the trees. Great Exceeding.
A realizing person establishes *himself* alone without fear.
A realizing person retires from the age without melancholy.

Transforming Lines

● **INITIAL SIX**
Offer a sacrifice using *a mat of* white thatch grass.
Without fault.

Prepare things very carefully. Be clear and pure, and concentrate on the essentials. This is not a mistake. The beginning is humble, but the result will be great.

● **NINE AT SECOND**
A withered willow gives birth to a shoot.
An older husband acquires a *younger* woman as consort.
There is nothing for which this is not advantageous.

Something is added to this worn-out situation that results in a burst of new growth. This will benefit everything. It connects what belongs together.

● **NINE AT THIRD**
The ridgepole buckles. The way is closed.

The structure of your life buckles and fails. The way is closed. There is nothing you can do to brace it up.

● **NINE AT FOURTH**
The ridgepole crowns *the house.* The way is open.
If there is more added, *there will be* shame and confusion.

The structure of your life is braced and strengthened. It is crowned with virtue and joy. The way is open. You have all you need. If you try to add more, you will simply confuse things and lose what you have.

● **NINE AT FIFTH**
A withered willow gives birth to flowers.
An older wife acquires a *younger* notable as husband.
Without fault, without praise.

Something is added to a worn-out situation that brings a brief burst of beauty. There is neither praise nor blame involved. Enjoy it. It cannot last for long.

● **SIX ABOVE**
If you exceed stepping into the water you will submerge the top
of your head.
Although the way closes, this is without fault.

These are deep and troubled waters and you must decide how far you want to involve yourself. If you go beyond simply stepping in, you will go under and be carried away. This is not a matter of fault or error, even though the way closes. There is something significant involved. Decide what action you want to take.

29 Repeating the Gorge

Unavoidable danger; take the plunge, face your fear; practise, confront something repeatedly.

• NAME

Repeat, HSI: practise, rehearse, train, coach; again and again; familiar with, skilled; repeat a lesson; drive, impulse. The ideogram portrays wings and a cap, thought carried forward by repeated movements.

Gorge, K'AN: a dangerous place; hole, cavity, pit, hollow; steep precipice; snare, trap, grave; a critical time, a test; take risks; *also*: venture and fall, take a risk without reserve at the key point of danger. The ideogram portrays a deep hole in the earth into which water flows.

• IMAGE

Repeating the Gorge.
There is a connection to the spirits.
Hold your heart fast, Success.
Moving will *bring you* honour.

This is a time of danger that you must confront. Take the risk without holding back. You cannot avoid the obstacle. It will repeat itself again and again. Conquer your fear. Practise, train, accustom yourself to the danger. This is a critical point that could trap you, so summon your energy and concentration. You have a connection to the spirits and they will help you. Hold your heart fast. Do not let it fall apart. Then you will have a strong centre. Moving into action and motivating things will bring you honour. Remember, danger has a purpose. Heaven uses danger to prevent ascending. Earth has its mountains and rivers. Kings use danger to guard their cities. A danger confronted is both an accomplishment and a defence. Now is the time to concentrate and take risks.

• OUTER AND INNER WORLDS: *Gorge* and *Gorge*.

The stream flows on, toiling and taking risks, levelling and dissolving differences.

• HIDDEN POSSIBILITY: *27 Jaws.*

Confronting danger and taking risks contain the hidden possibility of providing nourishment for yourself and others.

• SEQUENCE

You are not allowed to complete exceeding.
Acknowledging this lets you use the Gorge.
Gorge implies falling.

• DEFINITION

Radiance is above and the Gorge is below.

• SYMBOL

Reiterating streams culminate. Repeating the Gorge.

Transforming Lines

- **INITIAL SIX**
Repeating the Gorge.
Entering into the recess in the Gorge.
The way is closed.

By responding to the same danger again and again, you get caught in a dead end, the pit of depression. This closes the way. Do not do it.

- **NINE AT SECOND**
Venturing into the Gorge.
Seek *and* acquire *through* the Small.

You venture into danger. Seek what you need by being small. Adapt to each thing. Set modest goals. Do not impose your will. Thus you can succeed.

- **SIX AT THIRD**
Gorge *after* Gorge is coming,
So soften your *desire* to venture *into danger.*
Do not enter into the recess in the Gorge.

Danger after danger confronts you, so relax and pull back for now. If you jump in, you will be trapped in the pit, a fatal diversion. Are you sure you know what you want? Think about your values.

- **SIX AT FOURTH**
A cup, liquor, a platter added, and using a jar.
Let in the bonds that originate from the window.
Completing this is without fault.

If you are trapped in the Gorge, do not fight it. Lay out an offering, the distillation of your efforts. The answer will come in through the window, like light on a dark situation. You are right at the border, the place where events emerge. Going through with this is not a mistake.

- **NINE AT FIFTH**
The Gorge is not over full.
It is merely already even.
Without fault.

Do not put in too much. Do not fill things to overflowing. Do not make a great effort. Be content with what is there. The water is already rising.

- **SIX ABOVE**
Tied with stranded ropes.
Sent away to the dense jujube trees (*for judgement*).
For three years' time you will acquire nothing.
The way is closed.

You are bound and sent off for judgement. You will do nothing worthwhile for three years. The way is closed. Why act like this? Why let go of the way?

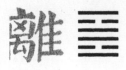

30 *Radiance*

Light, warmth and spreading awareness; join with, adhere to; see clearly.

- **NAME**
Radiance/clarity, LI: spreading light; illuminate, discriminate, articulate, arrange and order; consciousness, awareness; leave, separate yourself from, step outside the norms; two together, encounter by chance; belong to, adhere to, depend on; *also*: brightness, fire and warmth. The ideogram portrays a magical bird with brilliant plumage.

- **IMAGE**
Radiance, Advantageous Divination.
Success. Accumulate female cattle. The way is open.

This is a time of warmth, light and awareness, a time to be gentle and clear. Illuminate, articulate, connect things. Bring together what belongs together. This will bring profit and insight. Your efforts will be successful if you accumulate the receptive strength that can carry burdens. The way is open. Make an intelligent effort. Spread your awareness, connect and illuminate things to the four corners of the earth. The sun and moon hold with heaven and illuminate it. The many plants hold with the earth and illuminate it. Brightening things again and again lets people correct them. This is how change occurs in this world.

- **OUTER AND INNER WORLDS**: *Radiance* and *Radiance*.
Growing light, warmth and awareness spread in all directions, bringing together those who belong together.

- **HIDDEN POSSIBILITY**: *28 Great Exceeding*.
Spreading clarity and awareness contains the hidden possibility of building up great power.

- **SEQUENCE**
Falling necessarily has a place to come together *again*.
Acknowledging this lets you use Radiance.
Radiance implies coming together.

- **DEFINITION**
Radiance *is* above and the Gorge *is* below.

- **SYMBOL**
Brightness doubled arouses Radiance.
The Great Person uses consecutive brightening to illuminate all four sides.

Transforming Lines

- **INITIAL NINE**
Treading, then polishing *it*.
Respect it! Without fault.

Polish and clarify the first steps. Respect things and inquire into motives, particularly your own. Get rid of your own faults first. Then there will be no mistake.

- **SIX AT SECOND**
Yellow radiance. The way is fundamentally open.

This shows light and power from the earth's centre. The way is fundamentally open to you. A great idea and a creative time are on their way.

- **NINE AT THIRD**
The setting sun's radiance.
You do not beat on a jar and sing, by consequence you lament as in great old age.
The way is closed.

You see things in the light of the setting sun. Instead of beating your drum and singing your songs, you sit there like a very old person lamenting all the terrible things that have happened. The way is closed. Why go on like this? Take a grip on things.

- **NINE AT FOURTH**
Assailing like this, it comes like this.
It burns like this.
It dies like this.
It is thrown out like this.

This is a flash in the pan, a brush fire. It comes on quickly, flares up, dies down and is thrown away. It does not have a place in your life.

- **SIX AT FIFTH**
Tears issue forth like a gushing *stream*.
Sadness *breaks out* in lamentations.
The way opens.

Cry and mourn over this as if the sorrow would never end. This mourning will open the way. You will regain the lost connection.

- **NINE ABOVE**
The king issues forth chastising.
Through this, there is excellence.
Sever the heads, do not catch the demons.
Without fault.

This is the time for aggressive measures. Through disciplining and ordering things, by setting out in a determined way, you will achieve excellence. When you attack, take what is important and let the rest go. This is not a mistake. The opposition will fall apart. This ushers in a time of great abundance.

31 *Conjoining*

Influence or stimulus to action, excite, mobilize; connection, bring together what belongs together.

• NAME
Conjoin, HSIEN: contact, influence, move; excite, mobilize, trigger; all, totally, universal, continual, entire; unite, bring together the parts of a previously separated whole; come into conjunction, as the planets; literally: a broken piece of pottery, the two halves of which were joined to identify partners.

• IMAGE
Conjoining, Success.
Advantageous Divination.
Grasping the woman opens the way.

This shows an influence that connects with you and excites you into action, an inspiration, attraction or sudden surge of energy that aims at bringing things together. This is the attraction between the sexes and between the spirit and the human. Reach out, join things together, let yourself be moved. This brings success, profit and insight. Act through the woman and the yin. Understand this power. Feel its influence. This will open the way. Conjoining is the way the world is made. What you feel is the sign of something great. It can give you a way to order your heart and move the hearts of others. Accept, understand and submit to the woman and the yin. This is how beings change and give birth and how the sages move people's hearts. Through this you can see what moves the hearts of everything in heaven and earth.

• OUTER AND INNER WORLDS: *Open* and *Bound*.
Inner accomplishment provides a foundation for outer stimulation and cheer.

• HIDDEN POSSIBILITY: *44 Coupling*.
Bringing things together contains the hidden possibility of a meeting of the two primal powers.

• SEQUENCE
There is Heaven and Earth, then there are the myriad beings.
There are the myriad beings, then there are woman and man.
There are woman and man, then there are husband and wife.
There are husband and wife, then there are father and son.
There are father and son, then there are leader and servant.
There are leader and servant, then there are above and below.
There are above and below, then there is a righteous place to polish the codes.

• DEFINITION
Conjoining *means* urging.

• SYMBOL
Above the mountain there are the mists.
The realizing person uses emptiness to accept people.

Transforming Lines

• INITIAL SIX
It conjoins your big toes.

*This impulse starts you walking. It comes from far away and is in its
beginning. Locate your purpose beyond yourself. This could be the beginning of
a general renewal.*

• SIX AT SECOND
It conjoins your calves.
The way is closed. Residing *in place* will open the way.

*This impulse seeks to move you quickly, to sweep you off your feet. It is not a good
idea. The way is closed. Stay where you are and it will open again.*

• NINE AT THIRD
It conjoins your thighs.
Hold on to your following.
Going brings shame and confusion.

*This impulse seeks to start you running after it. Hold on to your desire and restrain
those who follow you. If you go on, it will only bring the shame and confusion of
having lost the way.*

• NINE AT FOURTH
Divination: the way is open, repenting disappears.
Wavering, wavering, coming and going.
Your partners will simply adhere to *your* pondering.

*A favourable influence. The way is open and your sorrows and doubts will
disappear. You go back and forth and the influence wavers. Think about it deeply
and friends and helpers will arrive. There is no harm in this connection, but your
central idea is not clear yet.*

• NINE AT FIFTH
It conjoins your neck.
Without repenting.

*A deep connection that will endure. You are feeling the tips of an impulse that will
manifest over time. This will bring no cause for regrets.*

• SIX ABOVE
It conjoins your jawbones, cheeks and tongue.

*This impulse conjoins your mouth and bursts forth in a torrent of words. They will
stimulate others, but the impulse will not last very long. When it ends, prepare to
pull back.*

32 *Persevering*

Continue on, endure and renew the way, constant, consistent, continue in what is right.

- ### NAME
Persevere, HENG: continue in the same way or spirit; constant, stable, regular; enduring, perpetual, durable, permanent; self-renewing; ordinary, habitual; extend everywhere, universal; the moon when it is almost full. The ideogram portrays a heart and a boat between two shores, enduring in the voyage of life.

- ### IMAGE
Persevering, Success.
Without fault.
Advantageous Divination.
It is advantageous to have a direction to go.

This is a time to continue on, to endure on your path and in what is right. Continue on as you are, and continually renew your decision. Be constant, regular and stable. Persist in your way of life or the thing you are doing. This is not a mistake. It will bring profit and insight. Have a definite direction or plan and follow it consistently. This is the way of the husband and wife, a relation that endures over time. Cling to established principles now. As you complete one thing, let it become the start of the next. The sun and moon depend on heaven, thus their light endures. The wise person endures in the way, thus the human world can change and perfect itself. If you contemplate where and how things persevere, you will see the deep purpose of all the myriad beings.

- ### OUTER AND INNER WORLDS: *Shake* and *Penetrating*.
Inner penetration and outer arousing continually renew
each other.

- ### HIDDEN POSSIBILITY: *43 Deciding*.
Lasting coherence contains the hidden possibility of clear and decisive action.

- ### SEQUENCE
The way of husband and wife does not allow not lasting.
Acknowledging this lets you use Persevering.
Persevering implies lasting.

- ### DEFINITION
Persevering *means* lasting.

- ### SYMBOL
Thunder and wind. Persevering.
The realizing person uses establishing, not versatility, on all sides.

Transforming Lines

• INITIAL SIX
Deepening persevering. Divination: the way is closed.
There is no advantageous direction.

You are going too deep, too soon and this closes the way. There is nothing you can do that will bring profit and insight. Let the situation grow and mature.

• NINE AT SECOND
Repenting disappears.

Continue on like this. Your doubts and sorrows will disappear. This brings you lasting ability, power and skill.

• NINE AT THIRD
Not persevering in your power and virtue.
Perhaps you receive *something, even then* you will be embarrassed.
Divination: shame and confusion.

You do not persevere in virtue. Even if you receive gifts you will be embarrassed by them, because you are being false to yourself. You feel the shame and confusion of having lost the way. Deliver yourself from this attitude.

• NINE AT FOURTH
The fields are without birds of prey.

There is no game here. Do not stay in this situation. Leave quietly and you will acquire what you need.

• SIX AT FIFTH
Divination: persevere in your power and virtue.
The way is open for the wife *and her* people.
The way is closed for the husband and the son.

Persevere in your virtue. This is a time of transition. You must choose how to act. If you choose the woman's way, the way is open to you. Adhere to what you are doing. If you choose the way of the man and his son, the way is closed. Cut yourself off from this situation and leave.

• SIX ABOVE
Rousing persevering, the way is closed.

Too much excitement and agitation. This closes the way. If a military man acted like this, he would soon lose all his troops. Rather than stirring things up, find an image for what is bothering you and seek a solution in the spiritual world.

33 Retiring

Withdraw, conceal yourself, retreat; pull back in order to advance later.

• NAME
Retire, TUN: withdraw, run away, escape, flee, hide yourself; disappear, withdraw into obscurity, become invisible; secluded, anti-social; fool or trick someone. The ideogram portrays a pig (sign of wealth and good fortune) and the sign for walk away. It suggests satisfaction, luck and wealth through withdrawing.

• IMAGE
Retiring, Success.
Advantageous divination *for* the Small.

This is a time to hide yourself, to withdraw from contacts and stay concealed. Acting in a small way will bring you success, so do not insist on your own ideas or try to have your way. Do not get emotionally entangled. In seclusion, you can prepare for a better time. You cannot stay where you are. Retire and be coupled with heaven. Decline involvements, refuse connections. Keep people at a distance not through hate but through a demanding integrity that inspires awe. Be adaptable. Immerse yourself in this situation and endure. Knowing when to retire is a very great thing.

• OUTER AND INNER WORLDS: *Force* and *Bound.*
An inner limit draws creative force into retirement from the world.

• HIDDEN POSSIBILITY: *44 Coupling.*
Withdrawing from involvements contains the hidden possibility of the conjunction of the two primal powers.

• SEQUENCE
You are not allowed to stay and last in your place.
Acknowledging this lets you use Retiring.
Retiring implies withdrawing.

• DEFINITION
Retiring, by consequence you withdraw.

• SYMBOL
Below heaven there is the mountain. Retiring.
The realizing person distances Small People.
The realizing person does not hate *them* but intimidates *them.*

Transforming Lines

• INITIAL SIX
The retiring tail, adversity.
Do not act, *but* have a direction to go.

You are caught and must go through the difficulty. Have a plan, but don't act on anything yet.

• SIX AT SECOND
Held by a yellow cow's skin.
Absolutely nothing can succeed in loosening it.

Held or holding on, this connection is absolutely secure. You must work with it.

• NINE AT THIRD
Tied retiring. *There is* affliction and adversity.
Accumulating servants *and* concubines opens the way.

Entangled in a web of difficulties and relations, you cannot retire. Use servants (who carry out orders) and concubines (who create a pleasant mood) to open your way.

• NINE AT FOURTH
Loving retiring.
The realizing person opens the way.
Small People *are* obstructed.

The way opens for the realizing person, who lovingly retires. This quality of selfless love blocks the way for those intent only on their own gain.

• NINE AT FIFTH
Excellence retiring. Divination: the way is open.

The way opens. As you retire, excellence comes with you.

• NINE ABOVE
Fertile retiring, there is nothing that is not advantageous.

Retiring will be of benefit to everything, enriching and fertilizing.

34 Great Invigorating

Great strength, the strength of the Great, have a firm purpose, focus your strength and go forward.

- **NAME**
Great, TA: big, noble, important; able to protect others; orient your will towards a self-imposed goal; the ability to lead your life; yang energy.
Invigorate, CHUANG: inspire, animate, strengthen; strong, flourishing, robust; mature, in the prime of life; *also*: damage, wound, unrestrained use of strength. The ideogram portrays a robust man, stout and strong as a tree.

- **IMAGE**
Great Invigorating, advantageous divination.

Great drive and power manifest themselves. Focus this strength through a central idea. Beware of hurting others by being excessive. This inner strength manifests itself directly, so come out of retirement and engage yourself. A strong creative force is stirring things up. You must be able to hold on to your strength. Correct one-sidedness in yourself and others. Having a great idea and correcting your own path lets you look into the heart of Heaven and Earth.

- **OUTER AND INNER WORLDS:** *Shake* and *Force.*
Great inner force is directly expressed through rousing action in the outer world.

- **HIDDEN POSSIBILITY:** *43 Deciding.*
Concentrating great strength contains the hidden possibility of clear and decisive action.

- **SEQUENCE**
You are not allowed to completely retire.
Acknowledging this lets you use Great Invigorating.

- **DEFINITION**
Great Invigorating, by consequence *you must* still *yourself.*

- **SYMBOL**
Thunder located above heaven. Great Invigorating.
The realizing person does not dispense with the codes, nowhere treading *outside them.*

Transforming Lines

• **INITIAL NINE**
Invigorating *strength* in the feet.
Chastising closes the way, there is a connection to the spirits.

Hold back and accumulate energy. Don't discipline people or set out on trips. That closes the way. The spirits are with you, but take your time.

• **NINE AT SECOND**
Divination: the way is open.

Act on your plan. All signs are favourable. This could begin a time of great abundance.

• **NINE AT THIRD**
Small People use invigorating *strength*.
The realizing person uses a net.
Divination: adversity.
The he-goat butts a hedge,
Entangling his horns.

Don't try to force your way. Use strategy and an empty centre. You are confronting difficulties that come from the past. Any use of force will simply get you entangled. Don't worry, the situation is already changing.

• **NINE AT FOURTH**
Divination: the way is open.
Repenting extinguished.
The hedge is broken through, *there is* no more entanglement.
Invigorating *strength* in the axles of a great cart.

The obstacle disappears, the way is open. Use your great strength to carry great things. This could begin a flourishing time.

• **SIX AT FIFTH**
Losing the goat to versatility.
Without repenting.

Change your driving strength to fluid imaginative power. Go with the flow. You will not be sorry about it.

• **SIX ABOVE**
The he-goat butts a hedge.
He is not able to withdraw and not able to release *himself*.
There is no advantageous direction.
Drudgery, by consequence the way opens.

You are temporarily entangled. You see no direction to move. You are in for a spell of hard work. This work will release you and open the way. A source of creative energy lies ahead.

35 *Prospering*

Step into the light, advance surely, receive gifts, be promoted, spread prosperity, dawn of a new day.

• NAME
Prosper, CHIN: grow and flourish, as young plants do in the sun; advance, increase, progress; be promoted, rise, go up; permeate, impregnate. The ideogram portrays birds taking flight as the sun appears at dawn.

• IMAGE
Prospering like Prince K'ang, you benefit from and bestow *gifts of horses to multiply the multitudes.*
In one day's sun, you are received three times.

You emerge slowly and surely into the full light of day, with the power to give and receive great benefits. This is a time to advance. You will be received by the higher powers. Be calm in your strength and poise, like Prince K'ang. Help things emerge and flourish. Give gifts of strength and spirit. The time has come to re-imagine yourself and your situation. Your strength has carried you forward. Continue to exert yourself. Further the development of all things. Step into the light. Join with others to brighten your great idea. Use the light given you to brighten the use of the tao.

• OUTER AND INNER WORLDS: *Radiance* and *Field.*
Light emerges from darkness and fertilizes the inner field, spreading prosperity to all.

• HIDDEN POSSIBILITY: *39 Difficulties.*
Flourishing and brightening contain the hidden possibility of re-imagining your difficulties.

• SEQUENCE
You are not allowed to complete invigorating.
Acknowledging this lets you use Prospering.
Prospering implies advancing.

• DEFINITION
Prospering *means* the day time.

• SYMBOL
Brightness issues forth above earth. Prospering.
The realizing person originates light to brighten power and virtue.

Transforming Lines

• INITIAL SIX
When you prosper, you are held back.
Divination: the way is open.
There is a net that connects you to the spirits.
You will be enriched without fault.

Don't worry about initial difficulties. The way is open. But use a net, not a weapon. The connection is there. Riches will come without fault.

• SIX AT SECOND
When you prosper, you are apprehensive.
Divination: the way is open.
Accept the close-woven chain mail and the blessing from your Queen Mother.

You are fearful, sorrowful or sad. Don't worry, the way is open to you. Accept what comes from the yin power. Even if it feels like constriction, it contains a blessing.

• SIX AT THIRD
The crowd is sincere.
Repenting disappears.

The crowds have confidence in you. There is no cause to hold back. Act wholeheartedly and have no fears.

• NINE AT FOURTH
You prosper, then *come* bushy-tailed rodents.
Divination: adversity.

Your prosperity attracts skulking animals that eat it up. This could be the return of angry ghosts and hungry memories. Strip away these old ideas. Be open to the new.

• SIX AT FIFTH
Repenting disappears.
Letting go or acquiring, have no cares.
Go *forward*, the way is open.
There is nothing that is not advantageous.

The way is open, go through with your plan. Have no worries about gain or loss. Everything will benefit from what you are doing.

• NINE ABOVE
Prospering with your horns.
Hold fast in order to subjugate the capital.
Adversity, the way is open, without fault.
Divination: shame and confusion.

Use your strength carefully. Hold on to it and subjugate your own capital. This means you must deal with your own ghosts. Acknowledge you have lost the right path. Have no fear. The way is open to this reformation. It will cleanse you of your faults.

36 *Hiding Brightness*

Hide your light, protect yourself, accept the difficult task.

- ### NAME

Brightness, MING: the light from fire, sun, moon and stars; consciousness, awareness, intelligence, understanding; illuminate, distinguish clearly; lucid, clear, evident; *also:* a bright bird, the golden pheasant. The ideogram portrays the sun and the moon. **Hide**, YI: keep out of sight; distant, remote; raze, lower, level; ordinary, plain, colourless; cut, wound, destroy, exterminate; barbarians, strangers, vulgar, uncultured people. The ideogram portrays a man armed with a bow.

- ### IMAGE

Hiding Brightness. Divination: drudgery is advantageous.

Hide your intelligence and awareness to protect yourself. Enter what is beneath you. This could be to avoid persecution or to accept a new and difficult task. There is a real possibility of injury here. By dimming your light you can avoid being hurt and find a release from your problems. Accept drudgery, hard work where you see yourself at a disadvantage as compared to others. This drudgery and difficulty will bring you profit and insight in the end. Hide yourself in common labour. Deliverance is already being prepared, so accept what confronts you. You are being excluded from the centre of things. Carefully watch the desires that connect you to others so you can control them. Brighten your innate pattern. Use the enveloping obscurity to clarify your worthy ideas. Accepting the drudgery and difficulty not only brings profit and insight. Knowing how to distinguish what is right in a dark time will make you an inspiration for others.

- ### OUTER AND INNER WORLDS: *Field* and *Radiance*.

Joining the common earth outside hides brightness and awareness within.

- ### HIDDEN POSSIBILITY: *40 Loosening.*

Dimming your intelligence contains the hidden possibility of being delivered from danger and tension.

- ### SEQUENCE

When you advance you will necessarily be injured.
Acknowledging this lets you use Hiding Brightness.
Hiding implies injury.

- ### DEFINITION

Hiding Brightness *means* being proscribed.

- ### SYMBOL

Brightness enters the earth centre. Hiding Brightness.
A realizing person supervises the crowds,
Using *both* darkening and brightening.

Transforming Lines

- **INITIAL NINE**

Hiding Brightness in flight.
You let your wings droop.
The realizing person when moving goes three days
without eating.
Have a direction to go.
The lordly person has words *to use.*

Hiding your brightness through taking flight. A weary time, three days without rest. Keep hold of your plan. Master your words to persuade others. The situation is already changing.

- **SIX AT SECOND**

Hiding Brightness. Hidden (*hurt*) in the left thigh.
Use a horse to rescue *him,* invigorating *strength* opens the way.

A serious but not deadly wound. Come to the rescue. Use the strength and speed of a horse. This will open the way. A flourishing time is not far ahead.

- **NINE AT THIRD**

Hiding Brightness in the Southern hunt.
You acquire their Great Head.
Divination: this does not allow affliction.

In the midst of difficulties you take the head of the leader of the opposition. In the end, this will cure all the pain and sadness that afflict you.

- **SIX AT FOURTH**

Enter into the left belly.
Catch the heart of the hidden brightness.
Issue forth from the gate and chambers.

You take the heart of the power oppressing you. Leave this place, this group, this way of thought. You have captured the meaning, so don't be sorry. A time of abundance is coming.

- **SIX AT FIFTH**

Prince Chi's brightness hidden.
Advantageous divination.

Prince Chi continued in his position while being oppressed without losing his integrity. He often had to resort to tricks and feigning. Such steadfastness will bring you profit and insight. Be clear about the real situation.

- **SIX ABOVE**

This is not brightening, but darkening.
Initially he mounted to heaven.
Afterwards he fell into the earth.

This plan doesn't brighten things, it darkens them. It is the place of the tyrant and oppressor. Whatever you are contemplating, don't do it!

37 Dwelling People

Hold together, an enduring group; adapt, nourish, support; family, clan.

• NAME
Dwell, CHI: home, house, household, family, relations, clan; a business; a school of thought; to be master of a skill or art; to hold something in common with others. The ideogram portrays a roof over a pig or a dog, the most valued domestic animals. **People**, JEN: human beings; an individual; humanity. The ideogram portrays a person kneeling in prayer or submission.

• IMAGE
Dwelling People. Divination: the woman is advantageous.

This is a group of people living and working together, a family or clan with ties of feeling between them. Care for your relationships with people, and the space you share with others. Profit and insight come through the woman and the yin. Accept, nourish, care for things. Thus warmth and clarity will spread throughout the dwelling and affect all the people. Dwelling means staying inside the net of feelings and relationships. Use your words to connect with people. A woman's attitude can correct the inside; a man's attitude can correct the outside. Together they reflect the great way of heaven and earth. Clarify each person's position so they know who and what they are. In this way, you can set the whole world right.

• OUTER AND INNER WORLDS: *Penetrating* and *Radiance*.
Warmth and awareness within bring people together through gentle outer penetration.

• HIDDEN POSSIBILITY: *64 Not Yet Fording.*
Being with people in a common dwelling contains the hidden possibility of collecting energy for an important new move.

• SEQUENCE
When you are injured outside, you necessarily turn back towards the dwelling.
Acknowledging this lets you use Dwelling People.

• DEFINITION
Dwelling People *means* the inside.

• SYMBOL
Wind originates from fire and issues forth. Dwelling People. The realizing person's words have being and his movement perseveres.

Transforming Lines

● **INITIAL NINE**
Through enclosing there is a dwelling.
Repenting disappears.

Fences, barriers, bars on the doors are what define a dwelling. Stay inside it. You will not be sorry. You are not ready to act yet.

● **SIX AT SECOND**
Release *what you have to give* without a direction.
Locate yourself in the centre and feed *the people.*
Divination: the way is open.

This is the place of the one who nourishes all the people in the dwelling, giving without imposing on others, providing for all. Act like this and the way will be open.

● **NINE AT THIRD**
Dwelling people, scolding, scolding:
Repenting and adversity open the way.
The wife and son, giggling, giggling:
Completing this brings shame and confusion.

This is a time for strict measures and discipline to put the house in order. If you let things go, you will lose the way.

● **SIX AT FOURTH**
An affluent dwelling, the Great way is open.

An affluent dwelling where the good flows for all. The way is certainly open. Let the flow of riches serve a real purpose.

● **NINE AT FIFTH**
The king imagines having a dwelling.
Caring for *other* beings opens the way.

The king's dwelling is a house of spirits that care for the many beings. Act from your heart. Mingle with others in mutual affection. The key to this royal dwelling is care for others.

● **NINE ABOVE**
There is a connection to the spirits that impresses *others.*
Completion opens the way.

Act on your idea. Carry it through. You are connected to the spirits. You will impress everyone you meet. The way is open.

38 Diverging

Opposition, discord; change conflict into creative tension through awareness.

• NAME
Diverge, K'UEI: separate, oppose, move in different directions; discord, conflict, distant, remote; animosity, anger; astronomical opposition, 180° apart yet connected on a common axis.

• IMAGE
Diverging, Small affairs open the way.

This is a time of discord and opposition. People move in different directions. Adapt to each thing and do not impose your will. This will open the way. It will enable you to clarify things and set them into creative tension. Diverging implies turning away. It is what is outside, strange and foreign. You must be able to both join things and separate them through brightness and awareness. For example, Heaven and Earth are opposed to each other, but they work together. Man and woman are opposed to each other, but their purposes come together. The myriad beings all diverge, but they are busy with the same things. Look at what connects and separates people. Then you can connect to what is truly great.

• OUTER AND INNER WORLDS: *Radiance* and *Open.*
The conflict between inner form and outer radiance is held in a creative balance.

• HIDDEN POSSIBILITY: *63 Already Fording.*
Discord and divergence contain the hidden possibility that the tensions are already resolved.

• SEQUENCE
When the way of dwelling is exhausted, you necessarily turn away.
Acknowledging this lets you use Diverging.
Diverging implies turning away.

• DEFINITION
Diverging *means* the outside.

• SYMBOL
Fire above, the mists below. Diverging.
The realizing person *both* concords and divides.

Transforming Lines

- **INITIAL NINE**

Repenting disappears.
If you lose a horse, do not pursue it, it will return by itself.
If you see hateful people, stay without fault.

Don't solve your problems by direct attack. You will not be sorry. What you have lost returns by itself. Stay unentangled. Don't be drawn into negative emotions.

- **NINE AT SECOND**

You meet *your* lord in the *narrow* street.
Without fault.

This is an important encounter with someone or something that can aid and guide you. There is no fault in acknowledging the connection.

- **SIX AT THIRD**

You see *your* cart pulled back, your cattle hampered,
Your people struck down and *their* noses cut off.
What you initiate will have no completion.

Your plans go astray. You meet unexpectedly strong opposition and what you started will not be completed.

- **NINE AT FOURTH**

Diverging alone.
You meet a fundamental *and* powerful man.
Mingling *together* connects you to the spirits.

Alone and isolated, you meet a powerful being. Connecting with this person will connect you to the spirits. What you have in your heart to do will come to pass.

- **SIX AT FIFTH**

Repenting disappears.
Your ancestor gnaws through the flesh!
How can this be a fault?

Your cares and sorrows will disappear. You partake of the sacrifice that connects you to the ancestors. Their power flows into you. How could this be a mistake?

- **NINE ABOVE**

Diverging alone, you see pigs bearing mud.
Carry *your* souls in one chariot.
At first you stretch the bow, then you loosen the bow.
They are in no way outlaws, seek matrimonial alliances.
In going you meet the rain, by consequence the way opens.

Alone and isolated, you see everything as filth. Get yourself together. At first you are hostile, later you will lay your hostility aside. The people approaching are not outlaws. Seek alliance with them. As you go on your way, the rain will wash away the conflicts. The way will soon be open.

39 Difficulties

Confront obstacles; feel hampered or afflicted.

• NAME
Difficulties, CHIEN: obstacles, obstructions, blocks, afflictions;
limp, walk lamely or haltingly; weak, crooked, unfortunate.
The ideogram: foot and cold, impeded circulation and a
wrong attitude.

• IMAGE
Difficulties. The southwest is advantageous.
The northeast is not advantageous.
It is advantageous to see the Great Person.
Divination: the way is open.

You are confronting obstacles and feel afflicted by them. Do not act. Re-imagine the
situation. Retreating and joining with others (in the southwest) brings profit and
insight. Don't go on your way alone and isolated or dwell on the past (northeast).
See important people who can help you to activate what is great in yourself. The way
is open to such activity. Though this is a difficult and arduous time, it contains the
possibility of renovating your inner power and your connection to
the way. Gather energy for a decisive new move. There is danger in front of you.
If you can see it and stop, you will really understand the situation. Correct the way
you use power and whom you depend on. By re-imagining your situation, you can
connect with what is truly great.

• OUTER AND INNER WORLDS: *Gorge* and *Bound.*
An inner limit blocks outer venturing, giving rise to reflection
and change.

HIDDEN POSSIBILITY: *64 Not Yet Fording.*
Re-imagining the situation contains the hidden possibility of
amassing the energy to ford the stream of events.

• SEQUENCE
Turning away is necessarily heavy.
Acknowledging this lets you use Difficulties.
Difficulties imply heaviness.

• DEFINITION
Difficulties *mean* heaviness.

• SYMBOL
Above the mountain there is the stream. Difficulties.
A realizing person reverses his personality to renovate *his* power
and virtue.

Transforming Lines

• **INITIAL SIX**
Difficulties going, praise *is* coming.

If you try to push on, you encounter difficulties. If you wait and open yourself to the new, praise will soon be there.

• **SIX AT SECOND**
The king's servant, difficulties, difficulties.
In no way is his person the cause.

You are pushing on against a sea of troubles and it is not your fault. You are in service of something greater than yourself. Continue on. Act as simply and clearly as possible.

• **NINE AT THIRD**
Difficulties going, the reverse *is* coming.

If you try to push on, you encounter difficulties. The situation will soon reverse itself. Stay inside and wait. You will soon have cause to rejoice.

• **SIX AT FOURTH**
Difficulties going, alliance *is* coming.

If you push on, you will encounter difficulties. The time that is coming will bring new connections and new events. This will be of real value to you. Open yourself to the influence.

• **NINE AT FIFTH**
In Great difficulties, partners come.

You are pushing on, focused on a great idea, encountering many difficulties. Don't worry, friends and companions will soon arrive to share the task.

• **SIX ABOVE**
Difficulties going, ripeness *is* coming.
The way is open.
It is advantageous to see the Great Person.

If you try to push on, you will encounter difficulties. If you wait and change your viewpoint you will meet greatness and eminence. The coming time is ripe and full. The way will soon open. Seeing people who can show you what is great in yourself will bring profit and insight.

40 *Loosening*

Solve problems, untie knots, release blocked energy; liberation, end of suffering.

• NAME
Loosening/deliverance, HSIEH: divide, detach, untie, scatter, sever, dissolve, dispel; analyse, explain, understand; free from constraint, dispel sorrow, eliminate effects, solve problems; discharge, get rid of; take care of needs. The ideogram portrays a sharp horn instrument used to loosen knots.

• IMAGE
Loosening.
The southwest *is* advantageous.
If you have no place to go, the return is coming, the way is open.
If you have a direction to go, *begin* at daybreak, the way is open.

This is a release from tension and difficulty. It brings rousing new energy. Untie knots, solve problems, free energy. Joining with others (the southwest) will bring profit and insight. If no problems confront you, simply wait for the energy to return. The way is open. If you have something left to do, do it quickly. This will bring achievement. The way is open. This is a very fortunate situation. Forgive and forget, enjoy the new freedom. Stir things up and let go of constraints. By going on, you can gather crowds around you. Heaven and Earth loosen things through thunder and rain, and the seeds of all plants burst forth. This is truly a great and arousing time.

• OUTER AND INNER WORLDS: *Shake* and *Gorge*.
Inside old structures are dissolving. This releases rousing new energy in the outer world.

• HIDDEN POSSIBILITY: *63 Already Fording*.
Loosening things and waiting for deliverance contains the hidden possibility that the action is already under way.

• SEQUENCE
You are not allowed to complete hardship.
Acknowledging this lets you use Loosening.
Loosening implies relaxing.

• DEFINITION
Loosening *means* relaxing.

• SYMBOL
Thunder and rain arousing. Loosening.
The realizing person forgives excess and pardons offences.

Transforming Lines

- **INITIAL NINE**

Without fault.

Act on your plan. You are in the right position, at the point where the
energy emerges.

- **NINE AT SECOND**

You catch three foxes in the fields.
You acquire a yellow arrow.
Divination: the way is open.

An omen of power. Foxes are crafty shape-changers, the yellow arrow a sign of
power from the earth. You acquire everything you need to act.

- **SIX AT THIRD**

Bearing *a burden* and also riding *in a carriage.*
This will involve outlaws in the end.
Divination: shame and confusion.

You are acting above yourself, and this invites danger. Take a good look at your
position and change it!

- **NINE AT FOURTH**

Loosening *your* thumbs.
Partners come in the end,
Splitting apart brings a connection to the spirits.

Break from what you usually depend on. New friends and helpers will come in the
end. The initial separation will connect you to the spirits.

- **SIX AT FIFTH**

When a realizing person is held fast, there will be loosening.
The way is open.
There is a connection to the spirits, move towards Small People.

If you trust the tao, you will find a way out of a difficult situation. Act like those
who adapt to what comes, without losing yourself.

- **SIX ABOVE**

A prince shoots a hawk on a high rampart above him.
He catches it. There is nothing that is not advantageous.

You can capture a tenacious opposing force and dissolve a pernicious influence.
Take careful aim. Everything will benefit from this.

41 Diminishing

Loss, decrease, sacrifice; concentrate, diminish involvements; aim at a higher goal.

• NAME
Diminish, SUN: lessen, take away from, make smaller; weaken, humble; damage, lose, spoil, hurt; blame, criticize; offer in sacrifice, give up, give away; let things settle; concentrate. The ideogram portrays a hand holding a ceremonial vessel, making an offering to the spirits.

• IMAGE
Diminishing, there is a connection to the spirits.
The way is fundamentally open.
Without fault, Divination: this is allowed.
It is advantageous to have a direction to go.
You ask how you can make use of it?
Two platters allow *you* to make a presentation.

Diminishing makes things smaller, higher, closer to the spirits and ideals. Gather your energy and send it upward. Withdraw from passionate and emotional involvements. Decrease personal connections. This fundamentally opens the way to you. This is an enabling divination. Have a plan and follow it. Inquire into your motivations. The two platters you use to make your presentation to the higher powers represent the increase of yin energy, the receptive, and the decrease of yang energy, the aggressive. This decrease is the necessary beginning of a new increase to come. The outer limit is there to bring inner development to expression. Something significant is returning. Let go of things. This is how you repair and adjust your relation to the way. It is heavy at first, but lets you be versatile and change with the time. Block the expression of anger and passion. This changes the flow of energy. Diminish what is below and augment what is above. Diminish the yang, augment the yin. This connects you to the time so that you can move with it.

• OUTER AND INNER WORLDS: *Bound* and *Open.*
An outer limit restricts involvement, stimulating inner development.

• HIDDEN POSSIBILITY: *24 Returning.*
Decreasing involvements and emotions contains the hidden possibility of returning to the origin.

• SEQUENCE
Relaxing necessarily lets things go.
Acknowledging this lets you use Diminishing.

• DEFINITION
Diminishing and Augmenting *are* the beginning of increase and decrease.

- **SYMBOL**

Below the mountain are the mists. Diminishing.
The realizing person curbs anger and restrains the passions.

Transforming Lines

- **INITIAL NINE**

Bring *your* affairs to an end and go swiftly.
Without fault. Discuss *how* to diminish it.

Leave what you are doing as swiftly as you can. Talk about how your involvement can be diminished. This is not a mistake.

- **NINE AT SECOND**

Advantageous divination.
Chastising closes the way.
This diminishes nothing, it augments *it.*

Whatever you are contemplating will bring you profit and insight. Do not try to discipline people or go on trips. This plan will not diminish you, it will augment you.

- **SIX AT THIRD**

When three people are moving, by consequence they will be diminished by one person.
When the one person is moving, by consequence he will acquire a friend.

This is a time to go by twos. If you are lonely, the friend will come. If you are part of a group, it will grow smaller.

- **SIX AT FOURTH**

Diminishing your affliction.
If you commission *someone* swiftly *to carry the message*, there will be rejoicing.
Without fault.

By doing this, your sickness, hatred and suffering will be diminished. Send the message quickly. It is not a mistake. It is a cause for rejoicing.

- **SIX AT FIFTH**

Perhaps ten pairs of tortoise *divinations* augment it.
Nothing can impede or contradict it!
The way is fundamentally open.

What a fortunate answer! Ten coupled divinations with the tortoise oracle would all agree. The way is fundamentally open. Nothing can contradict it or get in your way.

- **NINE ABOVE**

This diminishes nothing, it augments *it*
Without fault. Divination: the way is open.
It is advantageous to have a direction to go.
You acquire servants *but* not a dwelling.

What you are contemplating will augment things. It is not a mistake, the way is open. Have a plan. You will acquire people to help you, but not a family or a house.

42 *Augmenting*

Increase, expand, develop, pour in more, a fertile and expansive time.

• NAME
Augment, YI: increase, advance, add to; benefit, strengthen, support; pour in more, superabundant, overflowing; restorative, fertile; useful, profitable, advantageous. The ideogram portrays a vessel overflowing with material and spiritual benefits.

• IMAGE
Augmenting, *it is* advantageous to have a direction to go.
It is advantageous to step into the Great River.

This is a time of increase, advance and development. Increase your involvements and pour in more energy. Have a plan and carry it out. It is a good time to begin a major project or new enterprise. All these things bring profit and insight. By diminishing things, you have brought about a flourishing new time. Enrich everything, give without limits, like the rising sun. Stimulate people. Correct excess and error, and do not forget to correct yourself. New energy is penetrating the world. Get rid of your old ideas. Increase and enrich things without setting limits. Stimulate people at their work. When heaven spreads out, earth gives birth. Together they increase and augment everything. If you reflect this, you can move with the flourishing time.

• OUTER AND INNER WORLDS: *Penetrating* and *Shake.*
Rousing energy from within penetrates and permeates the outer world.

• HIDDEN POSSIBILITY: *23 Stripping.*
Increase and expansion contain the hidden possibility of stripping away what is outmoded.

• SEQUENCE
Diminishing without a climax necessarily augments *things.*
Acknowledging this lets you use Augmenting.

• DEFINITION
Diminishing and Augmenting *are* the beginning of increase and decrease.

• SYMBOL
Wind and thunder. Augmenting.
The realizing person sees improvement, by consequence he shifts *himself.*
The realizing person has an excess, by consequence he amends *it.*

Transforming Lines

• INITIAL NINE

It is advantageous to arouse and activate the Great.
The way is fundamentally open, without fault.

Rouse yourself to begin great efforts. This is not a mistake. The way is fundamentally open, even though your position is lowly and your resources slim.

• SIX AT SECOND

Perhaps ten pairs of tortoise *divinations* augment it.
Nothing can control or contradict it!
Divination: the way is perpetually open.
The king makes presentations to the Supreme, the way is open.

Ten coupled divinations with the tortoise shell oracle would all agree. The way is and will remain open for you. Nothing can contradict it or get in the way. This is the time of the great sacrifices, so offer your energy to the highest powers within you. The way is open for great things.

• SIX AT THIRD

Augmenting affairs *when* the way is closed.
Without fault.
There is a connection to the spirits, the centre is moving.
Inform the prince, use the sceptre *to speak.*

You are augmented through unfortunate affairs. This is not a mistake. The centre of things is moving and you are connected to it. The spirits are with you. Use your place or office to speak directly to the powers involved.

• SIX AT FOURTH

The centre is moving.
Inform the prince and adhere *to him.*
It is advantageous to act *on things* that depend on shifting the city.

The centre is changing. Tell the people in power and stay connected. Become involved in the move. Make it your centre of attention. This brings profit and insight.

• NINE AT FIFTH

You have a connection to the spirits and a benevolent heart.
Do not question *it,* the way is fundamentally open. *Say it thus:*
A connection to the spirits and a benevolent heart are my power
and virtue.

Act through your virtue and kindness. The spirits are with you. Do not question it. The way is fundamentally open. This connection and benevolence are the way you realize yourself.

• NINE ABOVE

This absolutely does not augment *you.* Perhaps it will smite *you.*
You establish your heart without perseverance. The way is closed.

An extremely unfortunate action. It can seriously injure you. You have not kept your heart firm, but waver without conviction. The way is closed.

43 Deciding

A critical moment, a breakthrough; decide and act clearly, clean it out and bring it to light.

• NAME
Decide, KUAI: choose; resolute, prompt, decisive, certain, clear; separate, fork, cut off, part, divide in two.

• IMAGE
Deciding, display *it* in the king's chambers.
There is a connection to the spirits, cry out *even if* there is adversity.
The information originates from the capital.
It is not advantageous to approach *with* arms.
It is advantageous to have a direction to go.

This is the moment to decide and then speak and act clearly upon your decision. Bring out what is hidden. Announce it even if it involves danger. Part from what is past. The information you now possess comes from a central source. Tell those who love or depend on you. It will bring you no advantage to resort to armed offence or defence. Having a clear plan to follow will bring profit and insight. Act with drive and persistence. The spirits are with you. Inner force comes to expression. Break through the obstacles. Help those who are below you. Keep your focus on the tao and never mind other considerations. The exposure to danger will make you shine in the end, but armed action will ruin everything. What is strong will endure, so bring your plan to completion.

• OUTER AND INNER WORLDS: *Open* and *Force*.
Inner struggle comes to clear expression in stimulating and inspiring words.

• HIDDEN POSSIBILITY: *1 Force*.
Deciding clearly and taking action contains the hidden possibility of great creative energy.

• SEQUENCE
Augmenting without a climax necessarily breaks through.
Acknowledging this lets you make use of Deciding.
Deciding implies breaking through.

• DEFINITION
Deciding *means* breaking through.
The strong breaks through the supple.

• SYMBOL
The mists lie above heaven. Deciding.
The realizing person spreads out benefits to extend to the below.
The realizing person resides in power and virtue and in consequence keeps aloof.

Transforming Lines

- **INITIAL NINE**
Invigorating in the advancing foot.
Going and not succeeding, a faulty action.

A bad start. Too much, too soon. This action cannot succeed. Stop now.

- **NINE AT SECOND**
Alarms and outcries.
Absolutely no *rest* at night.
Have no cares.

A tense situation, there are alarms at all hours. Have no cares, you will win through and obtain what you want. This can lead to revolution, renewal, a surge of creative energy.

- **NINE AT THIRD**
Invigorating in the cheek bones.
This closes the way.
The realizing person, deciding, deciding.
He goes alone *and* meets the rain.
He is indignant as if he were soaked.
Without fault.

You meet cruel people who insist on their mastery. Associating with them will close the way. Trying to decide what to do, you are caught in the rain and soaked with abuse. This is not your fault. Search out others who can feel with you.

- **NINE AT FOURTH**
The sacrum without flesh.
You also move *your* resting place.
If you haul the goat along, repenting will disappear.
When you hear words, do not trust them.

Hurt or punished, you are moving the place you rest. If you keep your capacity to act directly, your sorrows will disappear. Do not trust everything people try to tell you. Wait for the right moment to act.

- **NINE AT FIFTH**
Reeds and highlands, deciding, deciding.
Moving the centre is without fault.

You must clearly decide between two alternatives. Do not be afraid to move on. Act decisively. You are connected to a creative force.

- **SIX ABOVE**
You do not cry out.
Completing *this* will close the way.

If you do not communicate about your situation the way will close. Tell people about it! Call out!

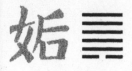

44 Coupling

Opening, welcoming, an intense personal encounter; meet and act through the yin, sexual intercourse.

• NAME
Coupling/Welcoming, KOU: meet, encounter, open yourself to; find something or someone on your path; the encounter of the primal powers, yin and yang; copulate, all forms of sexual intercourse; magnetism, gravity, mating of animals, gripped by impersonal forces; fortuitous; favourable, good. The ideogram portrays sexual intercourse.

• IMAGE
Coupling, the woman invigorates.
Do not act, grasp the woman.

A time to welcome what comes to you. Acting through the woman and the yin brings invigorating strength. Welcome what comes. Do not try to enforce your will. This is a time of meetings, brief, intense encounters that involve universal forces. Do not try to control things directly, but realize what happens to you reflects the union of these powers. Great things are moving in these events. The spirit spreads throughout the world. You are coupled with a creative force. It brings unexpected encounters, lucky coincidences and enjoyable happenings. Do not try to hold on to things. These contacts come and go. When Heaven and Earth meet, all the beings join in a brief radiant display. The time of welcoming and coupling is truly great.

• OUTER AND INNER WORLDS: *Force* and *Penetrating.*
Primal forces couple in the inner world, seeding a new generation. This is the axis of yin and yang.

• HIDDEN POSSIBILITY: *1 Force.*
The intensity of coupling contains the hidden possibility of great creative power.

• SEQUENCE
After breaking through there will necessarily be meetings.
Acknowledging this lets you make use of Coupling.
Coupling implies meetings.

• DEFINITION
Coupling *means* meeting.
The supple meets the strong.

• SYMBOL
Below heaven there is wind. Coupling.
The crown prince spreads his mandates to command the four sides.

Transforming Lines

- **INITIAL SIX**

Attached to a metal chock.
Divination: the way is open.
If you have a direction to go you will see the way close, *like* an
entangled pig who drags his hoof connecting to the spirits.

*Movement stops but the way is open. If you act on a plan, the way will close. You
will be like a little pig with a lame hoof chasing after the spirits. There is something
important in the standstill. Find out what it is.*

- **NINE AT SECOND**

Enwrapped *with* fish *inside*.
Without fault.
Hospitality is not advantageous.

A womb pregnant with coming abundance. Do not be or accept a guest.

- **NINE AT THIRD**

Your sacrum is without flesh.
You are also moving your rest house.
Adversity.
Without the Great *there will be* fault.

*Hurt or punished, you are moving where you rest. You will encounter dangers and
angry memories. If you do not have a central organizing idea, you will be in trouble.*

- **NINE AT FOURTH**

Enwrapped *with* no fish *inside*.
Rising up closes the way.

*An empty womb. This is not the time to act or object to things. Gently penetrate to
the core of the problem.*

- **NINE AT FIFTH**

Using osier to wrap melons.
A containing composition tumbles down, originating
from heaven.

*A containing elegance tumbles down from its source in heaven. A wonderful and
creative time is coming. Make it one with your own purpose. You can turn the world
into imagination.*

- **NINE ABOVE**

Coupling *with* your horns.
Shame and confusion.
Without fault.

*You are making an encounter into a trial of strength. Become aware of it and turn
back to the way. Then you will be without fault.*

45 *Clustering*

Gather, assemble, collect, bunch together, crowds; a great effort brings great rewards.

- **NAME**

Cluster, T'SUI: gather, call or pack together; tight groups of people, animals and things; assemble, concentrate, collect; reunite, reassemble; crowd, multitude, bunch; dense clumps of grass. The ideogram portrays a bunch of grass and a servant. It suggests gathering the capacity to do things.

- **IMAGE**

Clustering, Success.
The king imagines there is a temple.
It is advantageous to see the Great Person. Success.
This is an advantageous Divination.
Use the great sacrificial victims, the way is open.
It is advantageous to have a direction to go.

This is a time to unite people and things through a common purpose in order to accomplish great works. The goal is a vision in the mind of the king, the highest principle, and all can work towards it. Seeing those who can point out what is great, in the world and in yourself, will bring profit and insight. Great ideas are needed now. The way lies open to success, maturity and prosperity. Make a great sacrifice to the project at hand. Have a plan and carry it out. These things bring profit and insight. Clustering means collecting people together. Common labour comes to expression. Anticipate dangers so you are not taken by surprise. The people gather around a strong central vision, like the king who imagines a temple. Yield to the mandate in the time and work with it. By contemplating how people come together, you can understand the motives of all the beings under heaven.

- **OUTER AND INNER WORLDS:** *Open* and *Field.*

An inner willingness to serve stimulates and brings people together in the outer world.

- **HIDDEN POSSIBILITY:** *53 Gradual Advancing.*

Gathering things together contains the hidden possibility of gradual advance towards a goal.

- **SEQUENCE**

Beings meet together and then assemble.
Acknowledging this lets you use Clustering.
Clustering implies assembling.

- **DEFINITION**

Clustering *means* assembling.

- **SYMBOL**

The mists lie above the earth. Clustering.

The realizing person eliminates arms to implement *things.*
The realizing person warns against *being* without precautions.

Transforming Lines

• INITIAL SIX
There is a connection to the spirits, but no completion.
Therefore *there is* disorder, then clustering.
Like an outcry, one grasp of the hand brings laughter.
Have no cares.
Going on is without fault.

You and the people you are allied with are connected to the spirits. Uncertain, you
alternate between disorder and togetherness. Have no fears. This group is meant to
be. One grasp of the hand brings you back together. Now go on. It is not a mistake.

• SIX AT SECOND
Protracting opens the way, without fault.
There is a connection to the spirits,
Therefore *it is* advantageous to make dedications.

Draw things out. This opens the way. You are connected to the spirits, so even small
offerings with slim resources bring profit and insight.

• SIX AT THIRD
When *there is* Clustering, then *there is* lamenting.
No direction is advantageous.
Going on *is* without fault.
The Small *has* shame and confusion.

As soon as you get together, there are sorrow and painful memories. There is nothing
you can do here. Go on alone. It is not a mistake. Trying to adapt to
the situation will only bring shame and confusion.

• NINE AT FOURTH
The Great way opens, without fault.

Act on your plan. The great way is open to you. There is no mistake.

• NINE AT FIFTH
In clustering you have a situation.
This is without fault, *but* there is no connection to the spirits.
It is fundamental to perpetually make divinations.
Then repenting will be extinguished.

You have a place in this group, but there is no connection to the spirits here. Try
hard to find it. Then all your doubts and sorrows will disappear.

• SIX ABOVE
Paying tribute, sighs, tears, moaning.
Without fault.

You are paying for this connection with sighs, tears and sorrow. It is not your fault.
You are surrounded by the wrong people.

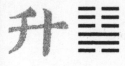

46 Ascending

Rise to a higher level, lift yourself, advance; climb up step by step.

• NAME
Ascend, SHENG: mount, go up, rise; climb step by step; advance through your own efforts; be promoted, rise in office; accumulate, bring out and fulfil the potential; distil liquor; an ancient standard of measure, a small cupful.

• IMAGE
Ascending, Fundamental Success.
Make use of and see the Great Person.
Have no cares.
Chastising *in* the South opens the way.

This is a time to move upward through your own efforts. Proceed step by step. Set yourself a goal and work towards it. This will give you a solid base and will bring great success. Put your purpose in order. Bring out the hidden potential. See people who can show you what is great in the world and in yourself, and use their influence. Have no cares or fears. You are undoubtedly on your way. Work hard. Set out towards the south, the region of summer, growth, intensity and action. The way is open to you. You can rise through inner adaptability. But it does not simply come to you. Work hard to realize the tao. *Amass small things to achieve the great. Penetrate to the core, for the centre of things is strong. Correct things, put them in order and set out on your way. Your purpose is indeed on the move.*

• OUTER AND INNER WORLDS: *Field* and *Penetrating*.
Inner penetration and subtle adaptation slowly ascend the outer field of activity.

• HIDDEN POSSIBILITY: *54 Converting the Maiden.*
Ascending contains the hidden possibility of realizing your own potential.

• SEQUENCE
Assembling and *moving towards what is* above imply the name Ascending.
Acknowledging this lets you use Ascending.

• DEFINITION
Ascending *means* it does not *simply* come *to you.*

• SYMBOL
Earth centre gives birth to wood. Ascending.
A realizing person yields to power and virtue.
A realizing person amasses the Small to use the high and the Great.

Transforming Lines

- **INITIAL SIX**
Sincere ascending. The Great way is open.

Your sincerity has been recognized and you are allowed to climb the sacred mountain. The way is open to your central idea.

- **NINE AT SECOND**
There is a connection to the spirits *so* it is advantageous to make dedications.

You are connected to the spirits. Making sacrifices even when resources are slim brings profit and insight. You will have cause to rejoice.

- **NINE AT THIRD**
Ascending *into* an empty capital.

Do not stop now. Have no doubts. Organize your forces and march on.

- **SIX AT FOURTH**
The king makes a sacrifice on the Twin-peaked Mountain.
The way is open.
Without fault.

The great sacrifices were for the good of all. Dedicate your efforts to the common good. The way is open to you. You will make no mistake.

- **SIX AT FIFTH**
Divination: the way is open, ascend the steps.

There are no barriers to your progress, but proceed step by step. The way is open to you.

- **SIX ABOVE**
Dark ascending.
Divination: *it is* advantageous not to pause.

Climbing on in the darkness, you cannot see where you are going. Do not stop. Go through it. That will bring profit and insight in the end.

47 *Confining*

Oppression, restriction, being cut off; the moment of truth; turn inward, find a way to open communication.

• NAME
Confine/oppression, K'UN: enclosed, encircled; restrict, limit; punishment, penal codes, prison; worry, anxiety, fear; fatigue, exhaustion, at the end of your resources; afflicted, disheartened, weary; poverty. The ideogram portrays a growing tree surrounded by an enclosure.

• IMAGE
Confining, Success.
Divination: the Great Person opens the way.
When there are words, do not trust them.

You are cut off, oppressed or exhausted and you cannot trust the people around you. You will have to master this situation from within. Gather your strength and wait for the moment to break out and break through. The only way out is to find the Great Person in yourself, where you are strong, clear and focused. That will open the way. Do not count on what other people tell you now, and do not trust words to communicate. If you have supportive friends, stay with them. Do not get caught in grudges or negative emotion. The purpose of this isolation is not to make you suffer, but to force you to find your individual connection to the way. There is a mandate for change hidden in the situation. It can show your your purpose. Think for yourself. Finding value in what your oppressors say will only exhaust you.

• OUTER AND INNER WORLDS: *Open* and *Gorge.*
Outer stimulation and contact are drawn into the inner stream, cutting off communication.

• HIDDEN POSSIBILITY: *37 Dwelling People.*
Isolation and oppression contain the hidden possibility of living and working with others in a common dwelling.

• SEQUENCE
Ascending without a climax necessarily confines *you.*
Acknowledging this lets you use Confining.

• DEFINITION
Confining *means* mutual meeting.

• SYMBOL
The mists without the stream. Confining.
The realizing person involves fate to release *his* purpose.

Transforming Lines

• INITIAL SIX
Your sacrum *is* confined (*punished*) with a wooden rod.
You enter into a shadowy gully.
For three years' time you will encounter no one.

Feeling hurt or punished, you hide yourself in melancholy and resentment. If you act like this you will be completely cut off from people.

• NINE AT SECOND
Confined while *drinking* liquor and eating.
Men wearing scarlet sashes are coming on all sides.
It is advantageous to make presentations and oblations.
Chastising will close the way, without fault.

This is the oppression of not being recognized, even though you have a comfortable life. The signs of praise are approaching. Make sacrifices to your ideals. That brings profit and insight. Disciplining people will close the way, even if you are in the right.

• SIX AT THIRD
Confined by stone. You lean on star thistles.
You enter into your house. You do not see your consort.
The way is closed.

Your feeling of oppression is completely wrong-headed. You lean on things that hurt you and cannot see the things that help. The way is closed to this sort of thinking.

• NINE AT FOURTH
Coming slowly, slowly, confined in a metal chariot.
Shame and confusion. There is completion.

The solution comes slowly, encased in bronze or gold. Through this you see you have lost the way. This lets you bring the situation to a successful end.

• NINE AT FIFTH
Nose cutting *and* foot cutting.
Confined by *a man with* a crimson sash,
Slowly there will be loosening.
It is advantageous to offer oblations.

This is oppression by authority. You have been punished and confined by someone official. This situation will slowly loosen of itself. Make offerings to your ideals.

• SIX ABOVE
Confined by trailing creepers,
By the unsteady and unsettled.
It is spoken thus: by stirring up repenting, there will
be repenting.
Chastising opens the way.

You are confined by things which are easily broken through. You are afraid to move. You just sit and lament. Rouse yourself. Put things in order. That opens the way. Do not just try to make everyone else feel guilty.

48 The Well

Communicate, interact, in good order; the underlying structure, network; source of life-water necessary to all.

• NAME
The Well, CHING: a water well; the well at the centre of a group of nine fields; resources held in common; underlying structure; nucleus; in good order, regularly; communicate with others, common needs; the water of life, the inner source. The ideogram is a group of nine fields with the well at the centre.

• IMAGE
The Well, amending the city does not amend the well.
Without loss, without acquiring, going and coming, the Well *is always* the Well.
A muddy end, not having a well-rope *in* the Well *or* ruining your pitcher:
These things close the way.

The well is both a social structure that lets people communicate and help each other and a deep source of life water there for all to draw on. You can do whatever you like or change the city you live in, but the needs represented by the well will never change. Lose or gain, come or go, the well and its water are always there. But if you let it turn to mud, if the rope is too short, if you do not have a container to hold it, then the way to the life water is closed. The well shows an end to confinement. It signals free communication and interpenetration between people. It is the earth that grounds the tao. Stay where you are and clarify your ideas of what is right. Work for the common good at humble tasks. The well nourishes all without being exhausted.

• OUTER AND INNER WORLDS: *Gorge* and *Penetrating.*
By repeatedly confronting outer danger you reach an inner ground where the water of life wells up.

• HIDDEN POSSIBILITY: *38 Diverging.*
The inner centre of the well contains the possibility of turning divergent opinions into creative tension.

• SEQUENCE
Confining above necessarily implies *that it is* reversed below.
Acknowledging this lets you use the Well.

• DEFINITION
The Well *means* interpenetrating.

- **SYMBOL**

Above wood there is the stream. The Well.
The realizing person toils for the commoners to encourage mutualizing.

Transforming Lines

- **INITIAL SIX**

This well is a bog, no one can consume *the water.*
An ancient well with no birds *who drink there.*

Time has left this well behind. It is of no use to anyone.

- **NINE AT SECOND**

This well is a gully *where* you shoot bass.
The jug is cracked and leaking.

There is nothing to contain the water from this well. Everyone is after his or her own ends. There is no connection between people.

- **NINE AT THIRD**

This well is unsettled and *its water* is not consumed.
This makes my heart ache,
For its water could be drawn
If the king were bright.
We could accept its blessing together.

This is the sorrow and heartache of ability that is not used. Water could be drawn from this well, but the king will not see it. Thus its blessing lies untouched. If you are in this situation, move on even if it is painful. Sooner or later your worth will be recognized.

- **SIX AT FOURTH**

This well is being lined, without fault.

A time of inner work and improvement. No water can be drawn for now, but this is not a mistake.

- **NINE AT FIFTH**

This well *has* cold, clear spring water to consume.

A pure, clear source. Use it freely and give thanks.

- **SIX ABOVE**

This well collects *all the waters* without a cover.
There is a connection to the spirits, the way is fundamentally open.

This well receives all and gives to everyone. Do not hide it. The way is fundamentally open to this capacity. By using this connection you can accomplish great things.

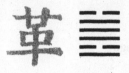

49 Skinning

Renew; moult, change radically, strip away the old, revolution, revolt.

• NAME
Skin/revolution, KO: take off the skin; moulting; radical change, renew; revolt, overthrow; skin, leather armour, soldiers; eliminate, repeal, cut off, cut away. The ideogram portrays an animal skin stretched on a frame.

• IMAGE
Skinning, on your own day there will be a connection to the spirits.
Fundamental Success: Advantageous Divination.
Repenting disappears.

This is the time when the snake sheds its skin, when radical change renews things. Strip away the old. Eliminate what has become useless so the new can be seen. Overthrow what is corrupt or decadent. On your own day, when the time is right, you will have a connection to the spirits. Act with confidence. This can inaugurate a whole new time. Success is guaranteed. It brings profit and insight. Reject old quarrels and memories. Present yourself in an entirely new way. Your doubts and sorrows will vanish. This is the time when heaven and earth renew themselves and great people carry out heaven's mandates. Yield and serve this great time.

• OUTER AND INNER WORLDS: *Open* and *Radiance.*
Changing inner awareness skins away obsolete forms to reveal a stimulating new potential.

• HIDDEN POSSIBILITY: *44 Coupling.*
Renewal through skinning contains the hidden possibility of a coupling of the two primal powers.

• SEQUENCE
The *tao* of the well does not allow you not to skin (*renew*) things. Acknowledging this lets you use Skinning.

• DEFINITION
Skinning *means* prior causes are leaving.

• SYMBOL
In the centre of the mists there is fire. Skinning.
The realizing person regulates how time is measured to brighten the seasons.

Transforming Lines

• **INITIAL NINE**
It is *tightly* secured in a yellow cow's skin.

You are tightly bound and cannot move yet. There is nothing you can do. Be open to the impulse when it comes.

• **SIX AT SECOND**
Your own day, therefore skin it! (*revolt*)
Chastising opens the way, without fault.

This is the time to revolt and renew things. Take action. Put things in order, and set forth. The way is open. The time is right. This is not a mistake.

• **NINE AT THIRD**
Chastising closes the way, Divination: adversity.
When skinning words draw near three times, *then* you will be connected to the spirits.

Now is not the time to set forth or discipline others. That closes the way. You are facing danger that has its roots in the past. Wait until the call to act comes three times. Then move on it. You will feel the connection and know what you are talking about.

• **NINE AT FOURTH**
Repenting disappears, there is a connection to the spirits.
Amend *heaven's* mandates, the way is open.

Act and have no doubts. You are called on to change the mandates of heaven. The connection to the spirits is there. The time is right. The way is open before you. All doubts and sorrows disappear.

• **NINE AT FIFTH**
The Great Person transforms *like a* tiger.
Even before the auguries, he is connected to the spirits.

When the time changes, Great People transform themselves like tigers. They move radically from one state to another. It does not take an augury to see what they have done. You are following a fundamental shift of ideas. Have no fear. Your own inner pattern will brighten the events.

• **SIX ABOVE**
The realizing person transforms *like a* leopard.
Small People *only* skin their face.
Chastising closes the way.
If you reside *in your place*, Divination: the way is open.

When the time changes, the realizing person changes with it like a leopard, moving with grace, elegance and power. Ordinary people simply change their face. Do not discipline people or set out on an expedition. If you remain where you are while you undergo this change, the way will be open. You will gather others around you.

50 *The Vessel*

Transformation, reach to the spiritual level; found, consecrate, imagine, contain.

• NAME

Vessel/Holding, TING: a cauldron with three feet and two ears, a sacred vessel for cooking offerings, sacrifices and ritual meals; founding symbol of a family or dynasty; receptacle; hold, contain and transform, transmute; consecrate, connect with the spirits; found, establish, secure; precious, well-grounded. The ancient ideogram portrayed questioning the spirits.

• IMAGE

The Vessel, the way is fundamentally open.
Success.

The Vessel represents transformation and connection to the invisible world. It gives you the capacity to change your situation through an image. You need to see deeply into your problem, to reflect and examine it until its spiritual meaning comes out. This will give you a new security. It fundamentally opens the way and assures you of success. Be resolute and break through old habits. By using the Vessel you can experience renewal. The Vessel means using symbols and becoming aware of their power. This brightens your understanding. Sages use this power to contact the great spirits and to nourish people of wisdom and worth.

• OUTER AND INNER WORLDS: *Radiance* and *Penetrating*.

Inner substance and penetration feed and spread the growing light of awareness.

• HIDDEN POSSIBILITY: *43 Deciding*.

Transforming things in the Vessel contains the hidden possibility of clear decisive action.

• SEQUENCE

Skinning (*transforming*) beings implies nothing like the Vessel. Acknowledging this lets you use the Vessel.

• DEFINITION

The Vessel *means* grasping renewal.

• SYMBOL

Above wood there is fire. The Vessel.
The realizing person corrects *his* situation to solidify *his* fate.

Transforming Lines

- **INITIAL SIX**
The Vessel *is* toppled over by the foot.
Advantageous: the obstruction issues forth.
This is like acquiring a concubine to make use of her son.
Without fault.

Something is blocking the process of transformation. You will have to turn things on their head to get rid of the obstruction, even if you go outside normal channels. This is not a mistake. It can usher in a very fertile time.

- **NINE AT SECOND**
There is something real in the Vessel.
My companion is afflicted *but* he is not able to approach me. The way is open.

There is something real in the Vessel, but your companions are full of disorder and hatred. Fortunately they cannot harm you. The way is open. Proceed on your own.

- **NINE AT THIRD**
The Vessel's ears *are* skinned.
Its movement is hindered.
The pheasant juice is not eaten.
Rain comes on all sides *and* lessens repenting.
Completing this opens the way.

Things feel clogged up and you cannot get a handle on it. You cannot get at the juice. Do not worry, it is part of a process that is changing the way you see things. The rain comes and washes away your doubts. Go through with this process. It opens the way.

- **NINE AT FOURTH**
The Vessel's stand *is* severed.
The prince's meal *is* overthrown *and* his form *is* soiled. The way is closed.

Whatever you are contemplating, do not do it. You would abandon your responsibilities and everything will be soiled. The way is definitely closed.

- **SIX AT FIFTH**
The vessel *has* yellow ears and metal rings.
Advantageous Divination.

Your plans are cooked, you have found the centre. You have a way to transport your insights. Act now. It will bring you profit and insight.

- **NINE ABOVE**
The Vessel *has* jade rings.
The Great way is open.
There is nothing that is not advantageous.

This is something truly precious, something that can focus and transform your entire life. The great way is open to you. Everything will benefit. This articulates a whole new world.

51 *Shake*

A disturbing and fertilizing shock; wake up, stir up, begin the new; return of life and love in spring.

• NAME
Shake, CHEN: arouse, inspire; wake up, shake up; shock, frighten, awe, alarm; violent thunder clap (thunder comes from below in Chinese thought), earthquake; put into movement, begin; terrify, trembling; majestic, severe; *also*: excite, influence, affect; work, act; break through the shell, come out of the bud. The ideogram portrays rain and the sign for exciting.

• IMAGE
Shake, Success.
The Shake comes, frightening, frightening.
Then come laughing words, shouting, shouting.
Though the Shake scares *people* for a hundred miles *around,*
He does not lose the ladle and the libation.

This is a disturbing and arousing shock, a burst of new energy. It brings new life and new love. Rouse things up to new activity. Re-imagine things. Let this shake up your old habits. When it first comes, the shock can be frightening. Then joy and laughter soon follow. The moment when the thunder first bursts from the earth in spring to revive everything and bring it back to life is a solemn moment. Do not be carried away. Focus on offering something to the spirits who have given us this joyous life. Inspect and adjust yourself. Act as a master of the ceremonies that bring fertility back to the earth.

• OUTER AND INNER WORLDS: *Shake and Shake.*
Sprouting energy thrusts up from below, stirring everything up to new growth.

• HIDDEN POSSIBILITY: *39 Difficulties.*
Rousing activity contains the hidden possibility of re-imagining a difficult situation.

• SEQUENCE
A lord's implements imply nothing like an elder son *to use them.*
Acknowledging this lets you use the Shake.
Shake implies stirring up.

• DEFINITION
The Shake *means* rising up.

• SYMBOL
Reiterating thunder. Shake.
The realizing person uses anxiety and fear to adjust and inspect *himself.*

Transforming Lines

• INITIAL NINE
The shake comes, frightening, frightening.
Then come laughing words, shouting, shouting.
The way is open.

First you are frightened, then you are glad. The anxiety will bring blessing in the end. Let the shock move you. The way is open.

• SIX AT SECOND
The shake comes *bringing* adversity.
A hundred thousand coins are lost.
Climb the ninth mound.
Do not pursue *what you have lost.*
On the seventh day you will acquire *it.*

The shock comes and takes everything you value. It seems as if all is lost. Do not run after it, do not be afraid. Climb the mound of transformation. When the time goes its full round, everything you lost will come back.

• SIX AT THIRD
The shake, reviving, reviving.
The shake moves without error.

The shock revives everything. Move with it. There is certainly no error here.

• NINE AT FOURTH
The shake releases a bog.

The shock is caught and everything bogs down. This impulse to action will trap you. Try to understand where this confusion comes from.

• SIX AT FIFTH
The shake comes and goes, *there is* adversity.
Do not lose your intentions and there will be affairs.

The shock comes and goes. There is danger with its roots in the past. Keep a firm hold on your purpose and you will have plenty to do.

• SIX ABOVE
The shake, twisting, twisting.
Observing *it,* terror, terror.
Chastising closes the way.
The shake is not in your body *but* in your neighbour's.
Without fault.
There will be words about matrimonial alliance.

The shock twists and turns, exhausting itself and winding people up in its coils. This is terrifying to see, but do not try to act. Do not be infected with this as your neighbour already is. Stay without entanglements. You will hear words about plans and alliances. Beware. There is a trap in this situation, but you can avoid being caught.

52 *Bound*

Calm, still, stabilize; limit or boundary, end of a cycle; become an individual.

• NAME
Bound/Stabilizing, KEN: limit, boundary, obstacle; still, quiet, calm, refuse to advance; enclose, mark off, confine; finish, complete; reflect on what has come before; firm, solid, simple, straightforward; the mountain as a limit and a refuge; *also:* stop, bring to a standstill. The ideogram portrays an eye and a person turning around to see what has led up to the present situation.

• IMAGE
Binding your back,
Not catching your personality.
Moving through your chambers not seeing your people.
Without fault.

Bound marks a limit, the end of a cycle, where things fully articulate themselves. They become individual. Calm and still your desire to act. Stabilize yourself. Do not try to advance, but see through your desires. By stabilizing your back, you still the personality. You can move through your life without being caught up in things or being confined to a social identity. This is not a mistake. It lets you calm and stabilize yourself. Stay where you are and think things over deeply. Recognize your limits. Stir things up or still them as the time requires, but do not get entangled with anything.

• OUTER AND INNER WORLDS: *Bound* and *Bound.*
Accomplishing words articulate what has been completed and suggest the new.

• HIDDEN POSSIBILITY: *40 Loosening.*
Stopping and accepting a limit contains the hidden possibility of being delivered from tension.

• SEQUENCE
Beings are not allowed to be completely stirred up.
Thus they are stilled.
Acknowledging this lets you use the Bound.
Bound implies stilling.

• DEFINITION
Bound *means* stilling *things.*

• SYMBOL
Joined mountains. Bound.
The realizing person ponders *and* does not issue forth from his situation.

Transforming Lines

• INITIAL SIX
Your feet are bound.
Without fault.
Divination: *this is* perpetually advantageous.

Action is stilled before it begins. This is not a mistake. This will bring you perpetual profit and insight.

• SIX AT SECOND
Your calves are bound.
You *can* not rescue your following.
Your heart is not glad.

Your forward motion is stopped. You are saved, but you cannot help those around you. This makes your heart ache.

• NINE AT THIRD
Binding yourself through restraints assigned to your loins.
Adversity smothers the heart.

This restraint is misplaced. You are cutting yourself in half. Acrid smoke and angry memories rise to smother your heart. Let go of this kind of binding.

• SIX AT FOURTH
Your personality is bound.
Without fault.

You still your own compulsive actions. This frees you from error.

• SIX AT FIFTH
Your jawbones are bound.
Your words will have order.
Repenting disappears.

You still the working of your mouth. This means that your speech will have order and elegance. Your sorrows and doubts will disappear.

• NINE ABOVE
Generous binding, the way is open.

The situation is bound with generosity, honesty and magnanimity. Use these qualities and you will meet them in others. The way is open.

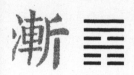

53 Gradual Advancing

Step by step, smooth, adaptable, penetrate like water; the oldest daughter's marriage.

• NAME
Gradual advance, CHIEN: advance by degrees, penetrate slowly and surely; infiltrate, adapt; flexible, supple, submissive; permeate, as water; influence, affect. The ideogram: water and cut through.

• IMAGE
Gradual Advancing, the converting (*marrying*) woman opens the way.
Advantageous Divination.

This is the time to gradually achieve a goal through adaptability and gentle, subtle penetration. The model is the marriage of the oldest daughter that proceeds slowly and ceremoniously. Do not take the initiative. Wait for the proper signs and signals to go forward. This gentle, adaptable yet penetrating attitude opens the way. It will bring you profit and insight. You will find the place where you belong and ultimately achieve mastery. It opens a new field of activity. Depend on your own moral strength and connection to the way to change the situation. Advance through the yin and the woman. Stabilize your desire, adapt and gently penetrate to the core of the situation.

• OUTER AND INNER WORLDS: *Penetrating* and *Bound*.
Inner stability provides the base for gradually advancing and penetrating the outer world.

• HIDDEN POSSIBILITY: *64 Not Yet Fording*.
Gradual advance contains the hidden possibility of amassing energy for an important move.

• SEQUENCE
You are not allowed to be completely stilled.
Acknowledging this lets you use Gradual Advancing.
Gradual Advancing implies advancing.

• DEFINITION
Gradual Advance *means* the converting (*marrying*) woman waits for the man to move.

• SYMBOL
Above the mountain there is the tree. Gradual Advancing.
The realizing person resides in eminent power and virtue to improve the vulgar.

Transforming Lines

- **INITIAL SIX**

The wild geese gradually advance to the barrier.
The small son *encounters* adversity, there will be words.
But this is lacking fault.

The first step. A young person confronts dangers from the past. You will be talked about, and you can use words to help you. Do not worry. This is not a mistake.

- **SIX AT SECOND**

The wild geese gradually advance to the stone.
There is drinking and eating, feasting, feasting.
The way is open.

A temporarily secure place on the journey, and a feast together with your companions. Enjoy yourself. The way remains open to you.

- **NINE AT THIRD**

The wild geese gradually advance to the highlands.
The husband is chastised and does not return.
The wife is pregnant and does not nurture.
The way is closed.
It is advantageous to resist outlaws.

A bitter place. People are divided against each other. The husband leaves, never to return. The wife ignores her children. This closes the way. Resist the temptation to behave violently and break rules. That brings profit and insight.

- **SIX AT FOURTH**

The wild geese gradually advance to the trees.
Perhaps they acquire their flat branch. Without fault.

A resting place after a transition. You do not really belong here, but you may find shelter for a while. This is not a mistake.

- **NINE AT FIFTH**

The wild geese gradually advance to the grave-mound.
The wife is not pregnant for three years' time.
When this is completed absolutely nothing can impede it.
The way is open.

The penultimate step. You connect with the ancestors and the seeds of new life. This will take time. When it is completed, nothing can stop it. The way is open. Go on.

- **NINE ABOVE**

The wild geese gradually advance to the highlands.
Their feathers allow activating the fundamental *rites and dances.*
The way is open.

The journey finds its goal in the realm above. The feathers float down and we can use them to contact the fundamental energies in our life. This symbolic connection will open the way for you again and again.

54 *Converting the Maiden*

Choice or transformation over which you have no control; realize your hidden potential; passion, desire, irregular progress; the younger daughter's marriage.

• NAME
Convert, KUEI: transform, reveal hidden potential, turn into; return to yourself or where you belong; restore, revert; loyal; give a young woman in marriage. The ideogram: wife and arrive, become mistress of the house.
Maiden, MEI: girl who is not yet nubile; younger sister, daughter of a secondary wife; person in a subordinate or servile position. The ideogram: woman and not-yet.

• IMAGE
Converting the Maiden, chastising closes the way
and leaves no advantageous direction.

You must go through a transformation that is beyond your control. In the end, it will reveal your hidden potential and open a whole new field of activity. The image of this is the marriage of the younger sister, who was often simply sent along with the elder, or a relationship that proceeds through passion, in fits and starts. This is now underway, but you can do nothing about it. Trying to impose order, or to leave the situation, would close the way. This transformation reflects a deep, perhaps unacknowledged need. Be receptive and adaptable. Act through the woman and the yin. This process is both an end and a new beginning. If Heaven and Earth did not mingle like this, the myriad beings would never emerge.

• OUTER AND INNER WORLDS: *Shake* and *Open*.
Rousing energy from outside realizes the inner potential to stimulate, inspire and give form to things.

• HIDDEN POSSIBILITY: *63 Already Fording.*
Standing on the threshold of events contains the hidden possibility of being already engaged in their solution.

• SEQUENCE
Advancing necessarily leads you to a place to convert (*marry*). Acknowledging this lets you use Converting the Maiden.

• DEFINITION
Converting the Maiden *means* a woman's completion.

• SYMBOL
Above the mists there is thunder. Converting the maiden.
The realizing person uses *what is* continuous and complete *in order* to know *what is* flawed.

Transforming Lines

• INITIAL NINE
Converting the maiden as a junior sister.
A halting gait *nevertheless* enables treading.
Chastising opens the way.

The woman marries as a junior wife, the lame man is able to go on his way. You are in a secondary position, but you can take effective action. Put things in order, discipline people, set out on your voyage. These things open the way.

• NINE AT SECOND
Squinting enables you to observe.
Divination: advantageous for shadowed people.

Look at things from an independent perspective. If you stay in the shade, hidden and secure, this will bring profit and insight.

• SIX AT THIRD
Converting the Maiden by growing a beard.
You reverse the conversion *if* you *play* the younger sister's *role.*

Use waiting and patience now. You will turn everything upside down if you hastily accept a subordinate position.

• NINE AT FOURTH
Converting the maiden by overrunning the term.
Procrastinating in converting *lets you find* the right time.

The accepted date has gone by. Let it go. Draw things out. This procrastinating will lead to the right time to act. A significant connection is approaching.

• SIX AT FIFTH
The Supreme Burgeoning converts the maiden.
His chief wife's sleeves were not as fine as her junior
sister's sleeves.
The moon that is almost full opens the way.

The Great Ancestor marries the maiden. An omen of great future happiness. What comes from the womb of the first wife is not as significant as what comes from the womb of the second wife. Accept the secondary position. Be like the moon that is not yet full. This is the story of the birth of three of China's great heroes. It is a very great omen for the future.

• SIX ABOVE
A woman receives a basket with nothing real *in it.*
A notable man disembowels a goat *sacrifice* with no blood *in it.*
There is no advantageous direction.

Everything here is an empty show. There is no sincerity or honesty. Nothing will bring profit or insight. Renounce this sterile situation.

55 *Abounding*

Culmination, plenty, copious, profusion; generosity, opulence, full to overflowing.

NAME
Abounding, FENG: abundant harvest; fertile, plentiful, copious, numerous; exuberant, prolific, at the point of overflowing; fullness, culmination; ripe, sumptuous, luxurious, fat; exaggerated, too much; have many talents, friends, riches. The ideogram portrays an overflowing vessel and sheaves of grain, a horn of plenty.

• IMAGE
Abounding, Success.
The king imagines this.
Do not grieve. The sun is properly at the centre *of the sky.*

A time of prosperity and great abundance, overflowing like the horn of plenty. Echo the abundance. Smile on everything, like the sun at midday. Overflow with good feeling, support and generosity. Imagine yourself as the king whose power bestows wealth and happiness on all. Such a time cannot last forever. When the sun reaches the centre it begins to set. When the moon is full, it begins to wane. Heaven and Earth fill and empty all things. But do not grieve about it. Put away your sorrow and melancholy. Shed light on all and eliminate the shadows.

• OUTER AND INNER WORLDS: *Shake* and *Radiance.*
Inner warmth and brightness permeate the world, rousing things up to abounding. These trigrams emphasize the fruits of completed actions.

• HIDDEN POSSIBILITY: *28 Great Exceeding.*
Generosity and abundance contain the hidden possibility of a great concentration of individual energy.

• SEQUENCE
Acquiring your place through converting (*marriage*)
necessarily implies the Great.
Acknowledging this lets you use Abounding.
Abounding implies the Great.

• DEFINITION
Abounding *means having* numerous previous causes.

• SYMBOL
Thunder and lightning culminate together. Abounding.
The realizing person uses severe litigation to involve punishment.

Transforming Lines

- **INITIAL NINE**

You meet your lord as an equal.

Although *you stay* a decade, *it is* without fault.

In going there is honour.

A fortunate meeting with someone who can help and teach you. You can stay with this person a whole period of time. This is not a mistake. Going on will bring honour.

- **SIX AT SECOND**

Abounding *is* your screen.

When the sun is at the centre *of the sky,* you see the Bin [*a constellation*].

Through going you will acquire doubt and affliction.

There is a far-reaching connection to the spirits.

The way is open.

You are screened off and protected. This lets you see hidden things. If you act on this directly, you will be greeted with doubts and hostility. Carry on. Your connection to the spirit world will carry you through. The way is open.

- **NINE AT THIRD**

Abounding *is* your profusion.

When the sun is at the centre *of the sky,* you see the froth *of stars.*

You break your right arm. Without fault.

Abounding spreads in all directions. You are overwhelmed by extraordinary sights. You lose your capacity to act. Do not worry. This is not a mistake. Even though you can do nothing, a fertile new time is on its way.

- **NINE AT FOURTH**

Abounding *is* your screen.

When the sun is at the centre *of the sky,* you see the Bin [*a constellation*].

You meet your hidden lord. The way is open.

You are screened and protected, and this lets you see hidden things. In this hidden place, you meet someone who can guide and teach you. The way opens before you.

- **SIX AT FIFTH**

A composition *is* coming.

There will be reward and praise, the way is open.

The next chapter in the book of life will be a beautiful composition. You receive rewards and praise for your efforts. The way opens before you.

- **SIX ABOVE**

Abounding is your roof.

You screen off your dwelling. You peep through your door.

You live alone, as one without *other* people.

For three years' time you will encounter no one.

The way is closed.

56 Sojourning

Wandering, living in exile, searching for your individual truth; outside the social net, on a quest.

• NAME

Sojourn/quest, LÜ: travel, journey, voyage; stay in places other than your home; temporary; visitor, lodger, guest; a troop of soldiers on a mission; a group (of travellers) that hold things in common or have a common goal; a stranger in a strange land. The ideogram portrays people gathered around a banner, loyal to a symbol of something distant.

• IMAGE

Sojourning, the Small *brings* Success.
Sojourning, advantageous Divination.

This is a time of wandering, seeking and living apart. You are a stranger in a strange land, whose identity comes from a distant centre. You can be successful by being small, adapting to each thing and not trying to impose your will. You are alone, outside the social network, with few connections, on a quest of your own. Consider things carefully. Make clear decisions even if they are painful. Limit and stabilize your desires when you are with others. By doing these things, you discover what you are seeking. In this way, the time of sojourning is truly great.

• OUTER AND INNER WORLDS: *Radiance* and *Bound*.

An inner limit provides a stable base for the sojourner's awareness of passing people and things.

• HIDDEN POSSIBILITY: *28 Great Exceeding.*

Wandering and searching contain the hidden possibility of a great build-up of energy.

• SEQUENCE

Exhausting the Great necessarily implies letting go your residence.
Acknowledging this lets you use Sojourning.

• DEFINITION

Connecting the few *is what* Sojourning *means.*

• SYMBOL

Above the mountain there is fire. Sojourning.
The realizing person brightens his consideration to punish *people* and not detain litigation.

Transforming Lines

- **INITIAL SIX**
Sojourning: fragments, fragments.
You split off your place and grasp calamity.

The voyage has no centre. The traveller is caught in meaningless details. You cut yourself off and reach out to disaster. Do you really want to act like this?

- **SIX AT SECOND**
The sojourner approaches a rest house.
Cherish your goods.
You acquire a young vassal.

You approach a place to stay. Be careful of what is yours. You will acquire help on your journey.

- **NINE AT THIRD**
The sojourner burns his rest house.
You lose your young vassal.
Divination: adversity.

The resting place burns and all help is lost. This is carelessness. It can truly involve injury. You are facing trouble with its roots in the past.

- **NINE AT FOURTH**
The sojourner abides in place.
You acquire goods and an emblem axe *and say*:
my heart is not glad.

You acquire an official position, a residence and goods. But deep in your heart this brings sorrow, not happiness. You have not found yourself here.

- **SIX AT FIFTH**
You shoot a pheasant – *with* one arrow it disappears.
Completing *this* brings praise and a mandate.

With a single shot you take the goal of your quest, something clever and beautiful. Go through with your plans. This will bring you praise and a mandate from above to carry out.

- **NINE ABOVE**
The bird burns its nest.
Sojourning people first laugh, then cry out and sob.
You lose *your* cattle to versatility.
The way is closed.

You are flirting with disaster. You may laugh now, but you will soon be crying. You will lose your home and all your goods. Whatever it is, do not do it! The way is definitely closed.

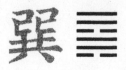

57 Gently Penetrating

Supple, flexible, subtle penetration; accept, let yourself be shaped by the situation; support or nourish from below.

• NAME
Gently Penetrating, SUN: penetrate, enter into, put into; supple, mild, subtle, docile, submissive; submit freely, be shaped by; support, foundation, base; *also:* wind, weather, fashion; wood, trees, plants with growing roots and branches. The ideogram portrays things arranged on a base that subtly penetrates them.

• IMAGE
Gently Penetrating, the Small *brings* Success.
It is advantageous to have a direction to go.
It is advantageous to see the Great Person.

This is the time for the pervasive influence of wind and growing roots and branches. Gently penetrate to the core of the situation. Be small, adaptable and subtle. Do not impose your will, but never lose your sense of purpose. This will bring success, profit and insight. Enter the situation from below and look to what is needed. See the people who can show you what is great in yourself and the situation. Balance and equalize things, but evaluate them in private. Be humble and hide your virtues. There is a strong purpose moving here and you can connect with it. Subtly penetrate it over time. Adapt to what crosses your path.

• INNER AND OUTER WORLDS: *Penetrating* and *Penetrating*.
Gentle penetration pervades inner and outer, matching and bringing them together as the start of a new generation.

• HIDDEN POSSIBILITY: *38 Diverging.*
Gently penetrating the situation contains the hidden possibility of turning divergent views into creative tension.

• SEQUENCE
You are sojourning and lack a tolerant place *to stay*.
Acknowledging this lets you use Gently Penetrating.
Gently Penetrating implies entering *a situation from below*.

• DEFINITION
Gently Penetrating *means* hiding *your influence*.

• SYMBOL
Following winds. Gently Penetrating.
The realizing person distributes his mandates to move affairs.

Transforming Lines

- **INITIAL SIX**
Advancing and withdrawing.
Act like a soldier to have an advantageous Divination.

Do not be indecisive. You may have to change directions many times, but act like a soldier and be firm whatever you do. If you hesitate, you undermine your own purpose.

- **NINE AT SECOND**
Gently penetrating beneath the bed.
Use historians and shamans.
What is mottled opens the way.
Without fault.

Get to the core of this old story. Use shamans, who can see spirits, and historians who know what happened in the past. What is mottled, that is, what partakes of both natural and spiritual realities, will open the way. Free yourself from fault by getting to the bottom of this situation and clearing it out.

- **NINE AT THIRD**
Urgent penetrating, shame and confusion.

Relax. You are pushing too hard. You will only confuse things and lose the way. Your purpose will be exhausted.

- **SIX AT FOURTH**
Repenting disappears.
In the fields you catch three kinds *of game.*

The field is open to action. Your doubts and sorrows will disappear. You will catch all you need. You are in a position to achieve something significant.

- **NINE AT FIFTH**
Divination: the way is open, repenting disappears.
There is nothing that is not advantageous.
But if you initiate *something,* it will not be completed.
Before you take the husk off, three days.
After you take the husk off, three days.
The way is open.

The way is open and your sorrows will disappear. Everything will benefit from this. Now is not the time to start something. Bring things to a successful conclusion. Watch carefully before and after you unveil the fruits of your labour. The way is open.

- **NINE ABOVE**
Gently penetrating below the bed.
You lose your goods and emblem-axe.
Divination: the way is closed.

Now is not the time to go into old quarrels and hidden things. You will lose your goods and your position. Let sleeping dogs lie. The way is closed.

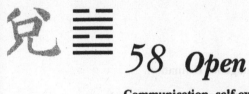

58 *Open*

Communication, self-expression; pleasure, joy, interaction; persuade, exchange, the marketplace.

• NAME
Open/expression, TUI: open surface, interface, interact, interpenetrate; express, persuade, cheer up, urge on, delight; pleasure, enjoy; responsive, free; gather, exchange, barter, trade; the words that come from the mouth; the fertilizing mists rising from a body of water. The ideogram shows a person speaking.

• IMAGE
Open, Success.
Advantageous Divination.

This is a time of communication, pleasure and free exchange with others. Express yourself openly. Cheer people on. Bargain, barter, exchange information. Free things from constraint. This is a time to see people and let yourself be seen. Join with friends to discuss and practise. Urge people on. Remember, if you explain things to people before they go to work, they will forget how hard the work is. If you explain why something is difficult or oppressive, they will even face death willingly. This is the power of stimulating words and a joyful, open presence.

• OUTER AND INNER WORLDS: *Open* and *Open*.
The open spreads everywhere, stimulating, cheering and revealing the form of things.

• HIDDEN POSSIBILITY: *37 Dwelling People.*
Open exchange and cheer contain the hidden possibility of the close relations between people who live in the same dwelling.

• SEQUENCE
You enter s*omething* and then stimulate it.
Acknowledging this lets you use the Open.
Open implies stimulating.

• DEFINITION
Open *means* seeing.

• SYMBOL
Congregating mists. Open.
The realizing person uses partners and friends to explain *things* repeatedly.

Transforming Lines

- **INITIAL NINE**
Harmonious opening, the way is open.

This is an opportunity for harmony to develop. The way is open to you.

- **NINE AT SECOND**
A connection to the spirits opens, the way is open.
Repenting disappears.

This connection opens the spirit world and gives you access to its energy and benevolence. The way is open. Your sorrows and doubts will disappear.

- **SIX AT THIRD**
A coming opening, the way is closed.

The opportunity that is coming up may look good, but there is nothing in it. Turn away. The way is closed.

- **NINE AT FOURTH**
Bargaining *about* opening is not yet soothed.
If you limit the affliction, there will be rejoicing.

There is still conflict and dissension over the terms of this connection. Do not let yourself get carried into negative emotions. The sooner you can clear this up, the better. Then you will have cause to rejoice.

- **NINE AT FIFTH**
A connection to the spirits through stripping away *the outmoded.*
There will be adversity.

A dangerous but very positive time. There is a connection to the spirit world and much energy available to you. But you must confront and strip away old ideas. Face things squarely. Correcting this situation is definitely the right thing to do.

- **SIX ABOVE**
Draw out the opening.

Draw things out by expressing your ideas. The situation is not clear yet. You do not have enough information to make a decision.

59 *Dispersing*

Dissolve, clear away, scatter, clear up; make fluid, eliminate obstacles and misunderstandings.

• NAME

Disperse, HUAN: scatter clouds, break up obstacles; dispel illusions, fears and suspicions; clear things up, dissolve resistance; untie, separate; change and mobilize what is rigid; melting ice, floods, fog lifting and clearing away. The ideogram portrays water and the sign for expand. It suggests changing form through expanding or scattering.

• IMAGE

Dispersing, Success.
The king imagines there is a temple.
It is advantageous to step into the Great River.
Advantageous Divination.

This is a time to eliminate misunderstandings and illusions and clear away obstacles. Let the light of understanding shine through. Be like the king who imagines having a great temple that can unite the people and connect them with the higher forces. Now is the time to start a project or found an enterprise. Enter the stream of life with a purpose. It will bring you profit and insight. Express yourself and spread clarity. This is the time when the early kings sacrificed to the highest powers. Clear away the fog, make yourself ready and go on to achieve something strong and great.

• OUTER AND INNER WORLDS: *Penetrating* and *Gorge*.

The inner stream penetrates the outer world, subtly dissolving and dispersing obstacles.

• HIDDEN POSSIBILITY: *27 Jaws.*

Dispersing obstacles contains the hidden possibility of providing nourishment for yourself and others.

• SEQUENCE

You stimulate *something* and then scatter it.
Acknowledging this lets you use Dispersing.
Dispersing implies radiance *breaking through.*

• DEFINITION

Dispersing *means* radiance *breaking through.*

• SYMBOL

Wind moves above the stream. Dispersing.
The early kings made presentations to the Supreme *power* to establish the temples.

Transforming Lines

• INITIAL SIX
Use a horse to rescue *this*, invigorating *strength* opens the way.

Something is in trouble. Rescue it with the strength of a galloping horse. This will open the way.

• NINE AT SECOND
Dispersing *by* fleeing your support.
Repenting disappears.

Leave what you usually depend on. This will bring clarity and disperse the obstacles. Your doubts and sorrows will disappear. You will get what you desire.

• SIX AT THIRD
Disperse your body.
Without repenting.

Do not identify with your desires, your need to express yourself, or your craving for personal power. Focus entirely on your purpose now. There will be no cause for sorrow.

• SIX AT FOURTH
Disperse your flock. The way is fundamentally open.
You disperse the *others* and *go to* the hill-top.
This is not at all hiding, it is a place to ponder.

Disperse those you usually associate with and go to the hilltop, where the ancestral graves lie, to ponder. The way is fundamentally open for you now. Do not think this is hiding. Use the time to connect with what is truly significant. The new time will come shining through.

• NINE AT FIFTH
Dispersing sweat, his Great outcry.
Dispersing the king's residence.
Without fault.

This is an order from on high. The king, the highest principle, is moving his residence and you must be part of the project. Work and sweat. Give your all. This is not a mistake. It will correct your situation.

• NINE ABOVE
Disperse the *bad* blood.
Leave, send it away, *then* issue forth.
Without fault.

Remove the possibility of conflict. Send anything that might cause quarrels or jealousy far away before you go out the door. This is not a mistake. Keep temptations at a distance.

60 *Articulating*

Give measure, limit and form; articulate thought and speech; rhythm, interval, chapter, units.

- **NAME**

Articulate, CHIEH: separate, distinguish and join things; express ideas in speech; joint, section, chapter, interval, unit of time, rhythm; the months of the year; limits, regulations, ceremonies, rituals, annual feasts; measure, economize, moderate, temper; firm, loyal, true; degrees, levels, classes. The ideogram portrays the nodes or joints on a stalk of bamboo.

- **IMAGE**

Articulating, Success.
Bitter articulating does not allow a Divination.

This is the time to give things limit and measure, to define connections. Separate and distinguish things. Above all, order your speech and express your thoughts. Create a whole in which each thing has a place. This means you must cut things to size and calculate the measures. Think about the way before you act. Apportion what is strong and what is supple. Harsh rules and bitter speech will cut you off from knowledge. Express things, take action, stay in the centre. By articulating the times and the measures, people and things are kept from harm.

- **OUTER AND INNER WORLDS:** *Gorge* and *Open.*

Stimulating words come from within to organize and articulate the stream of events.

- **HIDDEN POSSIBILITY:** *27 Jaws.*

Discriminating and articulating contains the hidden possibility of providing nourishment for yourself and others.

- **SEQUENCE**

You are not allowed to be completely radiant.
Acknowledging this lets you use Articulating.

- **DEFINITION**

Articulating *means* stilling *things.*

- **SYMBOL**

Above the mists there is the stream. Articulating.
The realizing person pares away *the unnecessary* to reckon the measures.
The realizing person deliberates power and virtue to move.

Transforming Lines

- **INITIAL NINE**

Do not issue forth from the *inner* door and chambers.
Without fault.

Stay inside. This restriction is not a mistake. It is not the right time to make contacts.

- **NINE AT SECOND**

Not issuing forth from the *outer* gate and chambers.
The way is closed.

Leave the way you usually act and think. Step out of your normal self or you will certainly regret it. The way will close to you.

- **SIX AT THIRD**

If it is not like articulating, it will be like lamenting.
Without fault.

If you do not articulate things and set limits, you will always be lamenting over painful memories. Whose fault is this confusion? Change and rid yourself of fault.

- **SIX AT FOURTH**

Quiet articulating, Success.

Articulate your ideas and your life quietly and peacefully. This will bring you success and the ability to inspire others.

- **NINE AT FIFTH**

Sweet articulating opens the way.
In going there will be honour.

Express yourself and order your life with sweetness, grace and delight. The way will open to you. As you go on in this way, you find honour and esteem. A significant connection is approaching.

- **SIX ABOVE**

Bitter articulating. Divination: the way is closed.
Repenting disappears.

Harsh measures and bitter speech. The way is closed. Let go of this idea unless you are truly desperate. It is like an animal gnawing its foot off to get out of a trap. Your doubts and sorrows will disappear.

61 Connecting to Centre

Connection to the spirit; just, sincere, truthful; the power of a heart free of prejudice; connect the inner and outer parts of your life.

• NAME
Centre, CHUNG: inner, central, calm, stable; put in the centre; balanced, correct; mediate, intermediary, between; the heart, the inner life; stable point that lets you face outer changes. The ideogram portrays an arrow fixed in the centre of a target.
Connect, FU: accord between inner and outer; sincere, truthful, verified, reliable, worthy of belief; have confidence; linked to and carried by the spirits; take prisoners, capture spoils, be successful. The ideogram portrays a bird's claw enclosing a young animal. It suggests both being protected and making a successful capture.

• IMAGE
Connecting to Centre, little pigs and fishes.
It is advantageous to step into the Great River.
Advantageous Divination.

This is a time to bring your inner and outer life together, to connect with the centre and the spirit. Be sincere, truthful and reliable. Recognize the inner connections between people and things. Empty your heart of greed, fear and desire, so you can see and hear the inner voices. This will bring abundance and fertility, signified by the little pigs and fishes. Enter the stream of life with a purpose, start a project, found an enterprise. This will bring you profit and insight. Let the expression of your inner connection permeate the world. Articulate it and trust it.

• OUTER AND INNER WORLDS: *Penetrating* and *Open.*
The open centre penetrates and links both inner and outer worlds.

• HIDDEN POSSIBILITY: 27 *Jaws*
Connecting to the centre contains the hidden possibility of providing nourishment for yourself and others.

• SEQUENCE
You articulate *something* and *then you* trust it.
Acknowledging this lets you use Connecting to Centre.

• DEFINITION
Connecting to Centre *means being* trustworthy.

• SYMBOL
Above the mists there is wind. Connecting to Centre.
The realizing person deliberates litigation to relax *the penalty of* death.

Transforming Lines

- **INITIAL NINE**
Taking precautions opens the way.
If there are others *involved, you will have* no peace.

Calm and stabilize yourself, so you are ready for whatever may come. If you are always thinking about others, you will have no peace. Concentrate on your own situation.

- **NINE AT SECOND**
A calling crane in the yin (*hiding*).
Its son is in harmony with it.
I have a beloved wine cup.
Associate with me, I will simply pour it out.

This is the profound echo of an immortal soul calling to its kindred, inviting them to a hidden feast. This call can transform your heart's desire. Do not hesitate to answer it.

- **SIX AT THIRD**
You acquire an antagonist.
Perhaps you beat a drum, perhaps you desist.
Perhaps you weep, perhaps you sing.

You acquire an equal antagonist, a hidden double. You sound the drums to attack, then stop. You weep, then you sing. Back and forth, there is very little you can do except leave the situation.

- **SIX AT FOURTH**
The moon *is* almost full.
The horse's yoke disappears.
Without fault.

The horse separates from its team-mates and goes its own way. The situation is almost at its peak. This is not a mistake. It can connect you with higher powers.

- **NINE AT FIFTH**
There is connection to the spirits that *creates* bonds.
Without fault.

Act on your ideas. There is a connection to the spirits here that will create ties between people on a deep level, as surely as links in a chain. This is definitely not a mistake. It is time to correct the situation.

- **NINE ABOVE**
A soaring sound mounts to heaven.
Divination: the way is closed.

This is empty, overly ambitious talk that flies above itself. Why go on like this? The way is firmly closed.

62 *Small Exceeding*

A time of transition, adapt to each different thing; be very careful, very small; excess yin.

• NAME
Small, HSIAO: little, common, unimportant; adapt to what crosses your path; take in, make smaller; dwindle, lessen; little, slim, slight; yin energy.
Exceed, KU: go beyond; pass by, pass over, surpass; overtake, overshoot; get clear of, get over; cross the threshold, surmount difficulties; transgress the norms, outside the limits; too much.

• IMAGE
Small Exceeding, Success.
Advantageous Divination.
This allows Small affairs, it does not allow Great affairs.
A flying bird *brings* the sound *when* leaving:
The above is not the proper *place*, the below is the proper *place*.
The Great way is open.

This is a time of transition. Be very careful and very small. Keep your power hidden by carefully adapting to each thing that crosses your path. Do not under any circumstances seek to impose your will. This will bring you success, profit and insight. It will carry you through the transition. Confine yourself to small things and stay below in any situation. This is not the time to try something important or to take the lead. Let the little bird tell you, your place is below. Do not go up, go down. By being exceedingly small and careful, the great way will open. Concentrate on the details.

• OUTER AND INNER WORLDS: *Shake* and *Bound.*
An inner limit holds and stills the rousing expression of inner energy.

• HIDDEN POSSIBILITY: *28 Great Exceeding.*
Small Exceeding contains the hidden possibility of a great concentration of energy.

• SEQUENCE
When there is trust *in something* it necessarily implies moving it.
Acknowledging this lets you use Small Exceeding.

• DEFINITION
Small Exceeding *means* excess.

• SYMBOL
Above the mountain there is thunder.
The realizing person in moving is exceedingly courteous.
The realizing person in loss is exceedingly mournful.
The realizing person in making use of things is exceedingly parsimonious.

Transforming Lines

• INITIAL SIX
Using a flying bird closes the way.

If you try to fly, you will close the way. Stay low and stay grounded.

• SIX AT SECOND
Exceed (*pass by*) your grandfather.
Meet your grandmother.
Do not extend *yourself* to your leader.
Meet his servant.
Without fault.

You do not meet the central figure, but the subordinate. This is not a mistake. Working from a secondary position is very effective. This connection will prove to have enduring value.

• NINE AT THIRD
You can nowhere exceed defending *yourself* against this.
If you adhere to this, perhaps you will be killed.
The way is closed.

You are over-reaching yourself and are in real danger. If you go on like this you may be killed. The way is closed. Abandon this way of proceeding.

• NINE AT FOURTH
Without fault.
You nowhere exceed meeting it.
The adversity that is *now* going is a necessary warning.
Do not perpetually try *what is past*.

There is no error in this situation. You meet what you need, the connection is made. Take a look at what has happened in the recent past, and let it be a warning to you. Do not always repeat the same mistake.

• SIX AT FIFTH
Shrouding clouds, no rain.
They originate from my Western outskirts.
A prince with a string-arrow grasps another in a cave.

The clouds gather, rolling in from the West, but no rain comes as yet. The culmination is very near. In this time of building tension, someone connects with you. This is a climax and an enduring connection. It will couple you with a creative force.

• SIX ABOVE
You meet it nowhere, you exceed it (*pass by*).
This is the flying bird's radiance. The way is closed.
This is called a calamity and an error.

You will not accomplish anything like this. You overreach yourself, flying higher and higher. The time is wrong and the way is closed. Do not act like this. You invite disaster from without and within.

63 *Already Fording*

Already underway, the action has begun; proceed actively, everything is in place and in order.

• NAME

Already, CHI: completed, finished; mark of the past tense; thus, that being so. The ideogram portrays a person kneeling in front of a bowl of food, already having begun the meal.

Ford, CHI: cross a river, overcome an obstacle, begin an action; give help, bring relief; succeed, bring to a successful conclusion, complete. The ideogram portrays water running over a flat bottom, a shallow fording place.

• IMAGE

Already Fording. Success *through* the Small.
Advantageous Divination.
Initiating *something* opens the way.
Completing *something brings* disorder.

The action is already underway. You are fording the stream of events. Everything is in the proper place and things are cooking. This is an advantageous situation and can bring profit and insight. You can be successful through the small, through adapting to each thing and not trying to impose your will. Stay with the process. Beginning things will open the way, but trying to bring things to completion only creates disorder. Keep putting your energy at the service of what is underway. Set things right. Think deeply about the problems and dangers confronting you in order to defend against them. You are in the right place. Carry on with the work.

• OUTER AND INNER WORLDS: *Gorge* and *Radiance.*
Inner awareness joins with the willingness to take risks in the outer world.

• HIDDEN POSSIBILITY: *64 Not Yet Fording.*
Crossing the stream of events contains the hidden possibility of continually accumulating energy.

• SEQUENCE
When there is an excess of beings it necessarily implies fording. Acknowledging this lets you use Already Fording.

• DEFINITION
Already Fording *means* setting *things* right.

• SYMBOL
The stream is located above the fire. Already Fording.
The realizing person ponders distress and provides for defending against it.

Transforming Lines

- **INITIAL NINE**

Pull your wheels back.

Soak your tail.

Without fault.

Do not start too soon. Hold back for now. This is not a mistake.

- **SIX AT SECOND**

A wife loses her veil.

Do not pursue *it*.

On the seventh day, you will acquire *it*.

Something valuable has been lost. Do not go after it. When the time comes around, you will find it again.

- **NINE AT THIRD**

The High Ancestor subjugates souls on all sides.

Three years revolve and he controls them.

Do not use Small People.

This is a great enterprise that will take a long time to complete. In the process you will confront your own ghosts and shadows. Keep your purpose. Impose your will. Be strong and untiring. In the end you will control the situation.

SIX AT FOURTH

Silk clothes in tatters, *this is* a token.

Be on guard *until* the day is complete.

Be careful! Even silk clothes can quickly turn to tatters. You are crossing the river in a leaky boat. Do not relax your guard for a moment.

- **NINE AT FIFTH**

The Eastern neighbour slaughters *many* cattle.

The *small but* dedicated offering of the Western neighbour is not like this.

Be real *and sincere*, accept your blessing.

Do not compare yourself with the rich. What is important here is sincerity. Be true to yourself and give of what you can. Then you receive the real blessings of the spirits.

- **SIX ABOVE**

You soak your head.

Adversity.

You are in too deep and have lost yourself. You confront danger with its roots in the past that you are in no position to deal with. Why go on like this?

64 Not Yet Fording

On the edge of an important change; gather your energy, everything is possible; wait for the right moment.

• NAME

Not yet, WEI: incomplete, doesn't exist yet; has not occurred (but will occur in the course of time). The ideogram portrays a tree that has not yet extended its branches.

Ford, CHI: cross a river, overcome an obstacle, begin an action; give help, bring relief; succeed, bring to a successful conclusion, complete. The ideogram portrays water running over a flat bottom, a shallow fording place.

• IMAGE

Not Yet Fording, Success.
A Small fox *and* a muddy ford.
If she soaks her tail *there is* no advantageous direction.

You are on the verge of an important change, about to make a significant effort. Do not do it yet. Gather your energy and be sure your plans are in order so you can make the crossing without getting stuck. This will bring you success. The small fox is a very careful and clever animal. She tries each step and can change quickly when necessary. Imagine you are the small fox and make yourself ready to adapt to whatever might happen. If the fox crosses the ford to the mud of the other bank, then falls and soaks her tail, there will be nothing that you can do. Consider and distinguish things. There are forces moving you into the right position.

• OUTER AND INNER WORLDS: *Radiance* and *Gorge.*

Inner risk holds outer radiance back, building up reserves of energy.

• HIDDEN POSSIBILITY: *63 Already Fording.*

Accumulating energy contains the hidden possibility of actually crossing the stream of events.

• SEQUENCE

Being is not allowed to exhaust itself.
Acknowledging this lets you truly and completely use
Not Yet Fording.

• DEFINITION

Not Yet Fording *means* masculine *drive* is exhausted.

• SYMBOL

Fire located above the stream.
The realizing person uses consideration
To mark off the beings *who* reside on all sides.

Transforming Lines

- **INITIAL SIX**
Soaking your tail.
Shame and confusion.

Too much, too soon. You are confused. You make it clear you do not understand.

- **NINE AT SECOND**
Pulling your wheels back.
Divination: the way is open.

Pull back, even though everything is loaded. Do not start yet. This opens the way and corrects how you are moving.

- **SIX AT THIRD**
Not yet fording, chastising closes the way.
It is advantageous to step into the Great River.

You are at the very edge. Do not try to discipline people or set out on expeditions. Step into the river with a clear purpose. This will bring you profit and insight.

- **NINE AT FOURTH**
Divination: the way is open, repenting disappears.
The *power of the* Shake subjugates souls on all sides.
When three years revolve there will be celebration in the
Great City.

This is a great enterprise. Act wholeheartedly. The way is open and your doubts and sorrows will disappear. Rouse and inspire your forces to subjugate the disorder and corruption of the demon's country. This will take a long time, but in the end you will be praised and honoured. There will be a great celebration of your victory. Your purpose is truly moving.

- **SIX AT FIFTH**
Divination: the way is open, without repenting.
This is a realizing person's shining.
There is a connection to the spirits, the way is open.

Act on your plans. The way is open and there will be no cause for regrets. This is the shining brightness of the one who truly follows the way. The spirits are in accord with you. The way is open.

- **NINE ABOVE**
There is a connection to the spirits in drinking liquor.
Without fault.
If you soak your head there is a connection to the spirits in
letting that go.

At the end of the crossing, people gather to celebrate and the spirits are there among them. Do not soak your head and lose yourself in the past. Feel the new time and let all that go.

Key to the Hexagrams

To find the hexagram that the Oracle has given you as an answer to your questions, locate the lower trigram on the left and the upper trigram on the top of the chart. Then turn to the hexagram text that the number indicates.

UPPER TRIGRAMS

LOWER TRIGRAMS

	FORCE	FIELD	SHAKE	GORGE
FORCE	1	11	34	5
FIELD	12	2	16	8
SHAKE	25	24	51	3
GORGE	6	7	40	29
BOUND	33	15	62	39
GROUND	44	46	32	48
RADIANCE	13	36	55	63
OPEN	10	19	54	60

				LOWER TRIGRAMS
BOUND	GROUND	RADIANCE	OPEN	
26	9	14	43	FORCE
23	20	35	45	FIELD
27	42	21	17	SHAKE
4	59	64	47	GORGE
52	53	56	31	BOUND
18	57	50	28	GROUND
22	37	30	49	RADIANCE
41	61	38	58	OPEN

Further Reading

The most comprehensive translation in English
Karcher, Stephen and Ritsema, Rudolf, *I Ching: the Classic Chinese Oracle of Change*, Element Books, Shaftesbury, 1994.

An informative and friendly version of the oracle, containing all the texts, old and new
Karcher, Stephen, *The Elements of the I Ching*, Element Books, Shaftesbury, 1995

An interesting new translation of the oldest parts of the book
Jing-Nuan, Wu, *Yijing*, Taoist Study Series, Washington, DC, 1991

The classic Neo-Confucian translation, with an introduction by C. G. Jung
Wilhelm, Richard and Baynes, Cary, *The I Ching or Book of Changes*, 3rd edition, Princeton University Press, Princeton, 1967

A new translation of the first and most influential Confucian rendering of the book
Lynn, Richard John, *The Classic of Change (as interpreted by Wang Bi)*, Columbia University Press, New York, 1994

A classic philosophical study
Wilhelm, Helmut, *Heaven, Earth and Man in the Book of Changes*, University of Washington Press, Seatttle, 1977

A superb article on the central treatise of the Ten Wings
Willard Peterson, 'Making Connections: Commentary on the Attached Verbalizations of the Book of Change', *Harvard Journal of Asiatic Studies*, 42/2, pp 67–112, June 1992

An in-depth look at divination, modern and historical
Karcher, Stephen, *An Illustrated Encyclopedia of Divination*, Element Books, Shaftesbury, 1997

Classic studies on Chinese history and ancient culture
Granet, Marcel, *Chinese Civilisation*, Routledge, London, 1930.

Maspero, Henri, *China in Antiquity*, trans. Frank A. Kierman, University of Massachusetts Press, Amhearst, 1978

A brief but interesting look at the depth psychological approach
Jacobi, Jolande, *Complex/Archetype/Symbol*, Princeton University Press, Princeton, 1974